MAKE it WORK!

NORTH AMERICAN
INDIANS

Andrew Haslam & Alexandra Parsons

Consultant: Anne Armitage, B.A.
The American Museum in Britain

TWO-CAN
in association with
WATTS BOOKS

First published in Great Britain in 1995 by
Two-Can Publishing Ltd
346 Old Street
London EC1V 9NQ
in association with
Watts Books
96 Leonard Street
London EC2A 4RH

A catalogue record for this book is available from the British Library.

Hardback ISBN: 1 85434 276 2
Paperback ISBN: 1 85434 277 0

Editor: Lucy Duke
Series concept and original design: Andrew Haslam
Design: Helen McDonagh
Assistant model-maker: Sarah Davies

Thanks also to:
Colin and Jenny at Plough Studios and models, Katherine Bee, Rachael Bee, Jonathan Bee, Cordel Ellis, Alex
Crowe, Chloe Parsons, Matthew Cassidy, Julia Head, Tim Head, Poppy Ashey, Emma Colley, Lauren Paxman

Photographic credits:
Eric and David Hosking: p4 (ml); Peter Newark's Western Americana: p8 (tr), p24 (tr), p45 (tl), p60 (t);
Smithsonian Institution, Museum of American History: p10 (tr), p16 (tr), p27 (tr), p30 (tr), p32 (tr), p34 (tr),
p43 (tr), p46 (tl), p54 (tr); Denver Art Museum: p18 (tr); Robert Harding: p61 (br); Phoebe A Hurst Museum of
Anthropology, The University of California at Berkeley: p26 (bl); American Museum of Natural History, courtesy
Department of Library Services: p35 (tl), p56 (bl); Range Pictures Ltd.: p4 (tr), p5 (bl), p5 (tr), p5 (br), p61 (tl);
Zefa: p39 (tr); Mel Pickering p60 (map)

All other photographs by Jon Barnes

Printed and bound by G. Canale & C. SpA, Turin, Italy

Hardback 2 4 6 8 10 9 7 5 3 1
Paperback 2 4 6·8 10 9 7 5 3 1

Contents

Words marked in **bold** in the text can be found in the Glossary.
Unfamiliar words in the text headings may also be
included in the Glossary.

Studying Indian life

All human beings need food and shelter to survive. They also need things to look forward to that give their lives hope and meaning. Throughout history, different groups of people around the world have come up with their own ways of meeting these basic needs. Studying past **civilizations** can tell us how people used the resources around them to build shelters, how they farmed or found food, and how they met their spiritual needs and hopes for a better future.

△ *This Crow Indian in Montana is decorating buffalo hides which were used for making dwellings (see page 17).*

△ *Shoshoni Indians of the Great Basin lived in fertile regions near the Grand Teton mountains.*

THE INDIANS were scattered over a vast country. It had a wide range of climates and **terrains**, from parched deserts in the Southwest to the frozen wastes of the North to the dense forests in the East. Those who lived in the Canadian Subarctic region had to deal with an even more extreme climate. We look at their lives, along with those of the people who lived even further north, in *Arctic Peoples*, another title in the Make it Work! History series.

TO HELP YOU study this vast area, with its wide range of different peoples, North America has been divided into seven climate regions. Each has a symbol which is used purely as a guide, when information relates to a group of people from a particular part of the country.

KEY TO THE SYMBOLS AND AREAS

 - the Plains

 - the Northeast

 - the Northwest

 - the Southwest

 - California

 - the Southeast

 - the Great Basin and Plateau

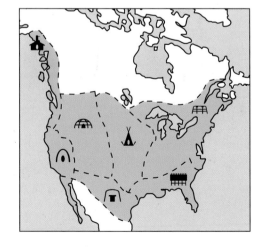

IN THIS BOOK we look at how the North American Indians lived from five hundred years ago, just before their traditional way of life was changed by the arrival of European settlers, to the present day. We can build up a picture of what this life was like from the tales told by the explorers and traders. These people were among the first from other parts of the world to have any contact with North American Indians. We can also learn a great deal from the stories that have been passed down from generation to generation by the Indians themselves. The studies of **archaeologists** and **anthropologists** are another source of information (see page 58).

△ *This Blackfoot Indian chief is painting pictures showing experiences in his life (see pages 50-51).*

THE TRADITIONS AND LIFESTYLES of North American Indians are a vital and living part of the country's history. They are kept alive by many of today's Indians who have chosen to live as their ancestors did. Other Indians prefer to live in a style that has different cultural roots.

▽ *These Plains Indians continue to live according to the traditions of their ancestors.*

THE MAKE IT WORK! way of looking at history is to ask questions of the past and find answers by making replicas of the things people made. However, you do not have to make everything in the book to understand the Indians' way of life. You should also realise that some of the objects included are based on sacred or ceremonial traditions. Therefore, they deserve the same respect as you would give to objects that are special to your own culture or beliefs.

▽ *The Iroquois Indians believed that these sacred masks gave the wearer the power to cure illnesses.*

Across the sea

Scientists believe that, over 50,000 years ago, the first people arrived in the continent that is now North America. They were **Ice Age** hunters from Siberia. They followed mammoth and giant bison south, as they searched the icy landscape for food. At that time, a huge area of ice formed a kind of bridge between Siberia and Alaska, so the hunters and their prey gradually moved from one continent to another. About 11,000 years ago, the world warmed up, this ice bridge sank and the countries were separated by what is now the Bering Strait.

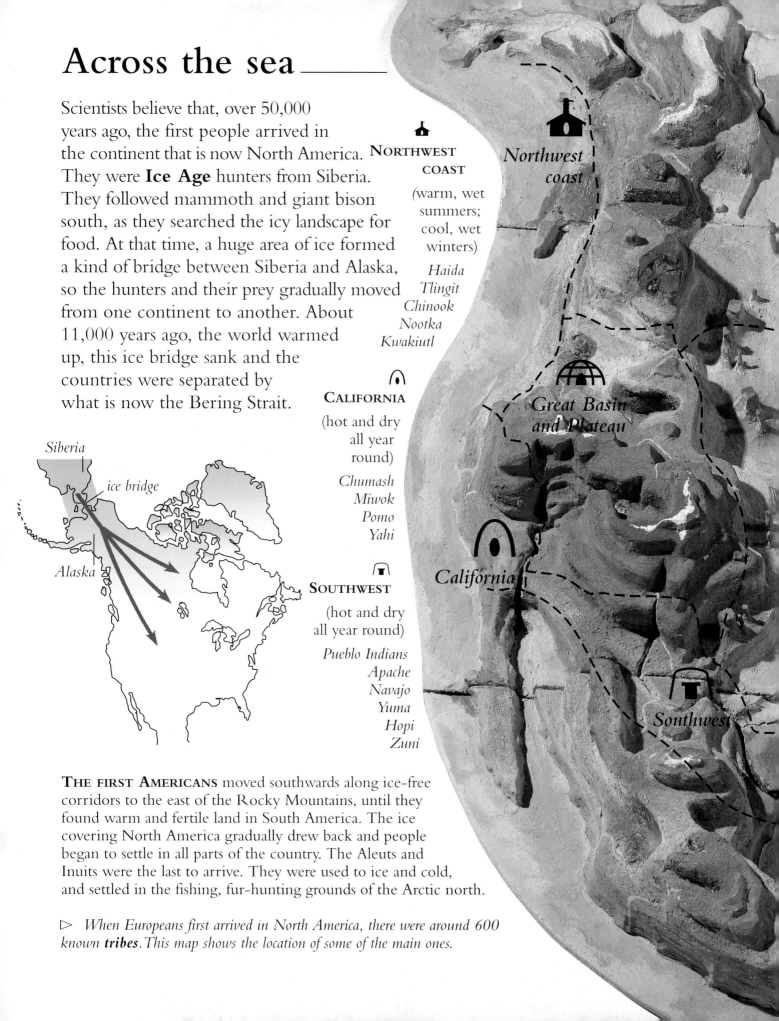

NORTHWEST COAST
(warm, wet summers; cool, wet winters)
*Haida
Tlingit
Chinook
Nootka
Kwakiutl*

CALIFORNIA
(hot and dry all year round)
*Chumash
Miwok
Pomo
Yahi*

SOUTHWEST
(hot and dry all year round)
*Pueblo Indians
Apache
Navajo
Yuma
Hopi
Zuni*

Siberia
ice bridge
Alaska

Northwest coast

Great Basin and Plateau

California

Southwest

THE FIRST AMERICANS moved southwards along ice-free corridors to the east of the Rocky Mountains, until they found warm and fertile land in South America. The ice covering North America gradually drew back and people began to settle in all parts of the country. The Aleuts and Inuits were the last to arrive. They were used to ice and cold, and settled in the fishing, fur-hunting grounds of the Arctic north.

▷ *When Europeans first arrived in North America, there were around 600 known **tribes**. This map shows the location of some of the main ones.*

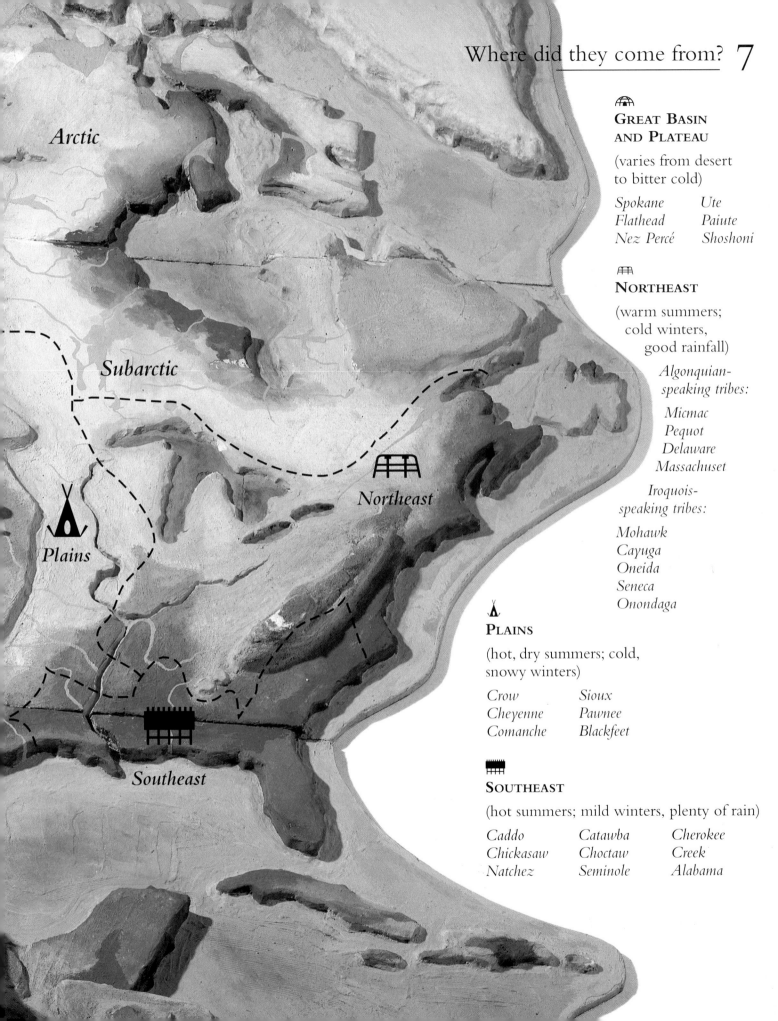

Arctic

Subarctic

Northeast

Plains

Southeast

GREAT BASIN AND PLATEAU

(varies from desert to bitter cold)

Spokane   Ute
Flathead   Paiute
Nez Percé   Shoshoni

NORTHEAST

(warm summers; cold winters, good rainfall)

Algonquian-speaking tribes:

Micmac
Pequot
Delaware
Massachuset

Iroquois-speaking tribes:

Mohawk
Cayuga
Oneida
Seneca
Onondaga

PLAINS

(hot, dry summers; cold, snowy winters)

Crow   Sioux
Cheyenne   Pawnee
Comanche   Blackfeet

SOUTHEAST

(hot summers; mild winters, plenty of rain)

Caddo   Catawba   Cherokee
Chickasaw   Choctaw   Creek
Natchez   Seminole   Alabama

Furs and feathers

Although many people think of traditional North American Indian dress as fringed tunics, feather headdresses and braided hair, this is not what everyone wore. It is the summer dress of some Plains tribes. The clothes people wore depended on where and how they lived, as with everything in American Indian life. Tribes in northern and eastern areas needed warm clothing. Many western and southern tribes wore very little, some decorating their bodies with tattoos. Hunting tribes made clothing from animal hides and fur, while gatherers and farmers used plant fibres.

△ *The first North American settlers were tall, well-built Siberian people, with broad faces, high cheekbones, straight black hair and brown skin.*

⚐ WARBONNETS were headdresses made from golden eagle feathers. Warriors proved their bravery by collecting feathers from the fierce, powerful birds. They cut and coloured them in different ways to let others know about their fighting skills (see page 46).

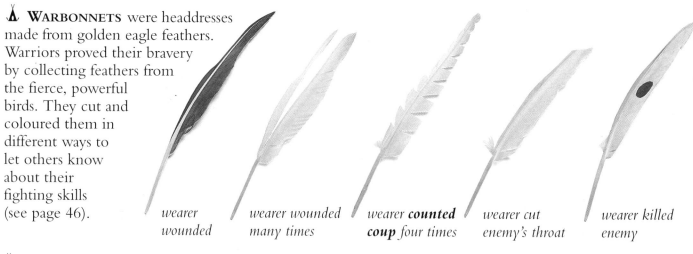

wearer wounded   *wearer wounded many times*   *wearer **counted coup** four times*   *wearer cut enemy's throat*   *wearer killed enemy*

⚐ MAKE A SIOUX HEADDRESS

You will need: canvas or other plain fabric, 12-15 feathers, coloured sticky tape, coloured ribbons, paint, paintbrush, scissors, Velcro, glue

1 Paint the tips of the feathers and wrap sticky tape around the quills.

2 Cut a canvas strip long enough to fit around your head with a good overlap and twice as wide as the headband will be. Turn in and glue the edges, then fold the strip in half lengthways. Mark and paint a design on it, as shown.

3 Glue inside the folded strip, leaving small, evenly-spaced pockets for the feathers. Glue a feather into each pocket. Decorate the headdress with coloured streamers made from the ribbons.

BODY PAINT made from reddish-brown mud called ochre, mixed with animal fat, was used by woodland tribes to paint their bodies. The designs and colours showed that people belonged to a special group, or told of their brave deeds or dreams. Body paint had a practical use, too. The grease in the paint protected skin from the sun, wind, cold, and from stinging and biting insects.

TATTOOS were worn by people in the hot, sunny Southeast and in California. They wore few clothes, and used tattoos to decorate and express themselves. They used needles made from cactus pins or slivers of bone to prick patterns on their skin.

HAIRSTYLES AND HEADGEAR were an important way to look different but still fit in with tribal traditions. Some groups smeared their hair with mud and sculpted it into elaborate shapes. Many warriors shaved their heads so they looked fierce and threatening. They sometimes tied a stiff tuft of animal hair, known as a **roach**, in the centre.

TWEEZERS made from shells, wood or bone were used by men to pluck hairs from their face. They rarely grew beards or moustaches.

HATS were made by many tribes, using the materials that came to hand. California Indians wove sun hats from reeds and decorated them with poppies. On the Northwest coast, hats were woven from cedar bark. Woodland tribes wore headbands made from fur or hide, or turban-like sashes woven from plant fibres.

4 Stick strips of Velcro on to the ends of the headband so you can fasten it around your head.

ⱶ **THE MEN OF THE GREAT PLAINS** wore only a piece of soft **buckskin** passed between their legs and tied with a belt. In winter, when the weather was fiercely cold, the men added fitted, thigh-length leggings and a knee-length tunic.

ⱶ **WOMEN'S LEGGINGS** were held up with garters just below the knee. Dresses were often made of two deerskins sewn together, with the animals' legs making natural sleeves. In the chillier north, both men and women wore robes made from softened buffalo skin with the hair left on.

ⱶ **CHILDREN** wore nothing in the summer, and child-sized versions of adult clothes in winter. Tunics, leggings and dresses were often decorated with quill-work or beaded embroidery.

△ *Ute warriors from the Great Basin and Plateau area wore magnificent breastplates of bone, porcupine quills and shells, and decorated themselves with body paint.*

ⱶ **MAKE A PLAINS OUTFIT**

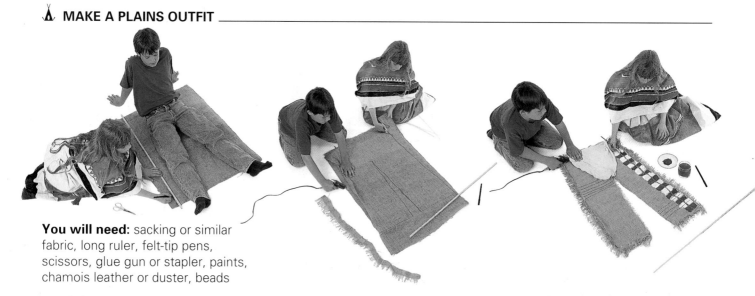

You will need: sacking or similar fabric, long ruler, felt-tip pens, scissors, glue gun or stapler, paints, chamois leather or duster, beads

1 To make the leggings, fold fabric in two and to make a rectangle. Measure and mark the trouser shape, as shown, using a long ruler or a straight piece of wood.

2 Cut through the two thicknesses of fabric. Glue or staple the seams (or sew them), adding strips of frayed fabric to the outer seams to look like fringes.

3 Paint designs directly on to the fabric, then glue or sew on a triangular duster, chamois leather or scrap of leftover fabric. This represents the buckskin loincloth.

△ *Clothes with a lot of beadwork were very heavy and were usually just worn for special occasions.*

ⱶ **ANIMAL SKINS** used for clothes had to be softened. This skilled work was done by women, who rubbed the skin with a mixture of animal brains, liver, ashes and fat. They soaked it in water and pulled, stretched or even chewed the leather until it became soft buckskin. Clothes made from skins were dry-cleaned by rubbing in clay and chalk to absorb the dirt.

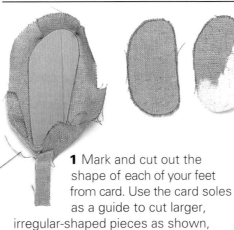

You will need: sacking or similar fabric, card, felt-tip pens, paints, thin string, a darning needle or bodkin

1 Mark and cut out the shape of each of your feet from card. Use the card soles as a guide to cut larger, irregular-shaped pieces as shown, then cut a toe piece and a thin strip.

2 Fold, and use string to sew the fabric around the cardboard soles, folding in the wings. Use the strip to join the two pieces at the heel.

3 Decorate the toe piece with paint or felt-tip pens.

4 Sew the toe-piece into position with string, as shown. Finish off your moccasins by stitching around the top edge, starting and finishing at the heel end. Then you can adjust the fit by tightening the string.

4 To make the tunic, fold a long piece of fabric into a rectangle, with the fold at the top. Measure and mark the shape, as shown, then cut it out through the two thicknesses of fabric. Cut a neck hole at the top. Glue, staple or sew the seams, as before.

5 Decorate your tunic with patterns, using paints or felt-tip pens. Add fringes, beads or feathers. You will find suggestions for designs and colours on page 37.

6 To make a woman's outfit, just make a long tunic (see page 13).

△ **MOCCASINS** were made in various styles for different uses. Some were low cut and others came almost to the knee. Work shoes had hard **rawhide** soles, while shoes worn at home were soft–soled. Moccasins helped protect people's feet from sharp stones, spiky plants, poisonous snakes and stinging insects.

▷ *Plains warriors carried spears and hide shields (see page 47) and wore elaborate headdresses (see pages 8-9).*

JEWELLERY AND ORNAMENTS were made from many different materials. Coastal tribes used shells, while Plains people used quills from birds' feathers and from porcupine spines coloured with vegetable and mineral dyes. Northern people had long been making copper necklaces, and once southern tribes had learned how to work silver, they made beautiful ornaments with bold tribal designs.

GLASS AND CERAMIC BEADS brought by Europeans were very popular because cutting, drilling and polishing stones and shells to make beads was hard work. The most important beads were **wampum**, made in the Northeast from ground, polished shells. They were used for decoration, keeping records, sending messages, making medicine and as money.

buffalo-horn helmet

ceremonial headdress

shell decoration

decorated goat-hair blanket

deerskin apron

woollen tunic

🏠 *Nez Percé*   〇 *Chumash*   🏠 *Tlingit*   🏠 *Navajo*

🏠 **THE NEZ PERCÉ** lived in high Plateau country to the west of the Rocky Mountains. The weather was cold and no crops grew. People relied on gathering roots, berries and nuts, and on fishing and hunting. Nez Percé warriors wore ermine-tail and buffalo-horn helmets, and buckskin war shirts with porcupine-quill decoration and horsehair tassels.

🏠 **THE TLINGIT**, like other Northwestern tribes, were wealthy and led comfortable lives. The winter months were a time of festivals and fun. Party outfits included blankets woven from goat hair and plant fibre tunics. It rained often, so people wore waterproof hats, tightly woven from spruce roots. Their tunics were good rainwear, too, drying out more quickly than a soggy deerskin ever could.

◖ **THE CHUMASH** lived near the Californian coast, in an area with plenty of food and a warm climate all year round. Women wore two deerskin apron-type garments around their waists. The back skirts were painted and decorated with shells, and the front aprons were fringed. Shoes were made of plant fibre. Women decorated their faces to show which family they came from.

▦ **MOHAWK WARRIORS** wore fringed animal hide cloths around their waists, with leggings and moccasins. They had tattoos on their foreheads that declared their bravery in battle, and sometimes wore fan-shaped roaches made of animal hair. Their war clubs were carved from a wood so hard that it was known as ironwood.

feather decoration

bead necklace

hide cloth

leggings

fringed tunic

⟁ *Plains*　　　▦ *Mohawk*　　　▦ *Seminole*

⬛ **THE NAVAJO** herded sheep, introduced by Spanish settlers, and therefore had access to wool. They wove blankets, often boldly striped and decorated with patterns unique to them. Women wore simple tunic dresses made from two pieces of blanket, tied at the waist with a woven sash. Leggings, soft moccasins, and beads and buckles of silver completed their traditional outfits.

▦ **THE SEMINOLE** were a group formed by Creek Indians and other people from different areas. They gradually came together in the Southeast after Europeans began to settle in North America. Their clothes were influenced by early European styles of dress, which they decorated with their own elaborate patchwork and beadwork.

Homes and shelters

The climate of the vast North American landmass varies between year-round snow and ice in the frozen North and scorching heat in the deserts of the Southwest. As the Indians settled into their homelands, they built houses and shelters that were suited to the climate and natural features of their particular region. They used whatever materials came to hand.

A LEAN-TO was a temporary shelter built by Subarctic peoples from sticks, leaves or bark.

A PLANK HOUSE was a winter home for the tribes of the Northwest. It was made from hand-split planks fixed on to a frame made from logs, and it was usually rectangular.

TEPEES were perfect homes for the **nomadic** buffalo-hunting Plains Indians. They were portable and were made of buffalo skins and wooden poles.

HOGANS were typical Navajo homes. They were hexagonal or octagonal in shape and were usually built facing east. They had a log and stick framework, plastered with mud and more wood or stones.

CLIFF DWELLINGS, or **pueblos**, were the homes of tribal groups in the Southwest, where humans have lived for at least 6,000 years and a settled farming culture thrived. Houses made of mud, rubble and blocks of stone built into rocky cliffs were called pueblos (meaning villages) by the Spanish, who arrived in the 16th century.

REED HOUSES were made from reed mats covering a wooden pole frame. Inside, there was often a central pit for a fire, with a smoke hole in the roof. These conical houses were often found in the Southwest and California.

IGLOOS are domed houses made from blocks of frozen snow. They were used as a temporary base during the seal-hunting season in the central Arctic region.

WICKIUPS were cone-shaped or domed houses built around frames made from wooden poles, often covered with grass or rush. They were the homes of many Great Basin people.

LONGHOUSES were the homes of the powerful and sophisticated peoples of the Northeast, who lived in fertile woodlands and prairies. They were built from timber and bark and housed up to 20 related families.

WIGWAMS were built by the **Algonquian tribes** in the Great Lakes area. They were made of wooden poles bent round to form arches and covered with mats of reeds and bark.

EARTH LODGES were made by piling earth over a frame made from large, long-lasting beams that could be re-used when a new home was built. They were built by the Navajo and by early farmers in the central Plains.

A CHICKEE was no more than a roof and floor on stilts. It was the summer home of tribes in the Southeast, who lived in villages ringed with secure barriers.

▲ **NOMADIC TRIBES** such as the Cheyenne and the Sioux spent much of their lives on the move across the central Plains following the buffalo, which were their main source of food. They were resourceful and clever people. Their tepees were pleasant, practical homes that were cool in summer, warm in winter, strong enough to stand up to fierce winds and big enough for the family and all their belongings.

▲ **TEPEES** were made from up to fourteen buffalo hides sewn together with buffalo sinews (the tough, stringy fibres that attach muscle to bone). Needles were carved from buffalo bone.

△ *These Comanche women, photographed in 1890, have pegged out buffalo skins so they can scrape them clean.*

▲ MAKE A TEPEE

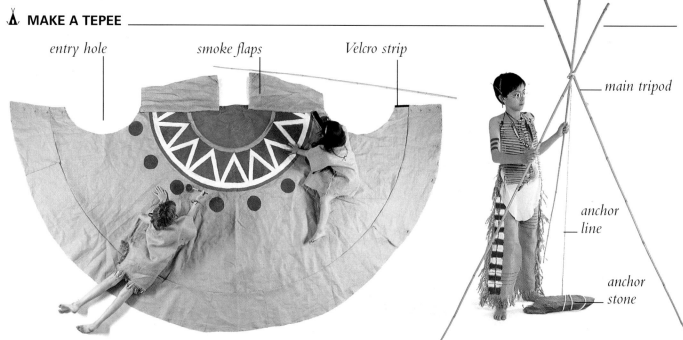

entry hole   smoke flaps   Velcro strip

main tripod

anchor line

anchor stone

You will need: hessian sacking 4.5 m wide and 2 m long, or old double sheets or blankets, drawing pin, string, scissors, garden canes, stapler or needle and thread, rope or washing line, paints, brushes, PVA glue, Velcro strip, short sticks

1 Cut a piece of string 50 cm shorter than your canes and use it like a compass to draw a semi-circle on the fabric. Pin one end to the centre of the long side of the fabric and tie a pencil to the other end. Swing the string round and mark an arc.

2 Cut small, matching semi-circular openings for the entry hole, as shown. Stick or staple strips of Velcro on either side of the hole for fastening the tepee over the canes.

3 Cut out the smoke flaps as shown and staple or sew them in place. Make a small triangular pocket in the top inside corner of each flap of the tepee cover (see step 7).

4 Paint the cover, adding PVA glue to the paint to make it waterproof. Use the scissors carefully to make holes for the tent pegs around the base.

5 Make the tepee frame using 3 canes. Tie them together, with the thicker ends at the top. Use a heavy object as a weight to secure the other end of the rope, as shown.

6 Wrap the cover carefully around the cane tripod and secure it by sticking the Velcro strips together. Plains Indians used tepee pins to hold the covers of their tepees in place. You can make your own pins using short sticks. Make holes in both layers of the tepee cover, where it overlaps, and thread the pins through the holes, as shown.

▲ **THE MAIN TRIPOD** was tied together on the ground, then heaved upright using an anchor line made from rawhide. A family tepee was usually five metres high and just under five metres in diameter, which is about as big as a medium-sized room.

▲ **SPECIAL PATTERNS AND COLOURS** were used by each tribe to paint their tepees. Families would adapt the tribal pattern for their own family. The number of dots, for instance, may have represented the number of lakes in the area. Women did the painting, using coloured soil mixed with buffalo blood and ground-up rock.

7 Slide more poles inside the tepee cover to make the frame stronger. Fix the base, using short sticks as tent pegs. Push one end of a cane into each smoke flap pocket to prop the flaps open. Finally, cut out and pin on a door flap to fit the entry hole.

▲ **ON RAINY DAYS** a tepee's smoke flaps were closed and fastened with tepee pins.

▲ **MEN AND WOMEN** had their own particular responsibilities. Women made and put up tepees, while men kept look-out. Two women would take about an hour to erect one tepee.

▲ **BLACK ELK**, a Sioux Indian, said: *"Our tepees were round like the nests of birds and these were always set in a circle, the nation's hoop, a nest of many nests where the Great Spirit meant for us to hatch our children."*

smoke flaps

entry hole

tepee cover

tepee pin

INSIDE THE TEPEE people slept on piles of warm, furry buffalo skins. When they gathered around the fire, they had comfortable wooden backrests to lean against. They stored their food, medicines and clothes in soft hide bags, embroidered with elaborate tribal patterns. A typical Plains Indian family had many horses but owned few possessions apart from the things they really needed.

TO PROVIDE EXTRA INSULATION against wind and cold, tepees often had decorative inner linings which trapped a pocket of warm air between the two layers to keep the inside temperature comfortable.

THE FIREPLACE, sometimes raised on a slab of stone, was the main source of light and heat. The supply of firewood was never allowed to run low.

WARNING: DO NOT LIGHT FIRES IN A MODEL TEPEE

△ *This soft buffalo-hide tepee liner belonged to a Cheyenne family. Tepee liners were not hung all around the tent, but were attached at the points where the wind whistled through, positioned at waist height to protect people from draughts as they sat around the fire or lay in bed.*

VENTILATION was provided during warm summer weather by rolling up the sides of the tepee to let the air in.

BACKRESTS were used only by the men of the family. The firm but springy supports were made of wooden slats lashed together with leather strips.

EVERYTHING HAD ITS OWN PLACE inside the tepee. The beds were placed on either side of the fire. The fire itself was set in front of the central anchor rope. Backrests were positioned against the sides and a supply of firewood was kept just inside the door.

▲ **A STRICT CODE** of manners meant that a Plains Indian could not just walk into a friend's tepee. There were rules to follow:

- If the door flap was open, visitors could enter, but if it was closed, they had to wait to be invited in.

- Male visitors went in first, moved around to the right and waited for the host to offer them a seat on his left. Women could then enter, and they turned left.

- Men were allowed to sit cross-legged, but women were not.

- Guests invited to a meal had to bring their own spoons and bowls and eat everything their host provided for them.

- No one was allowed to walk between the fire and another person.

- When the host lit his pipe, it was the signal for the guests to go home.

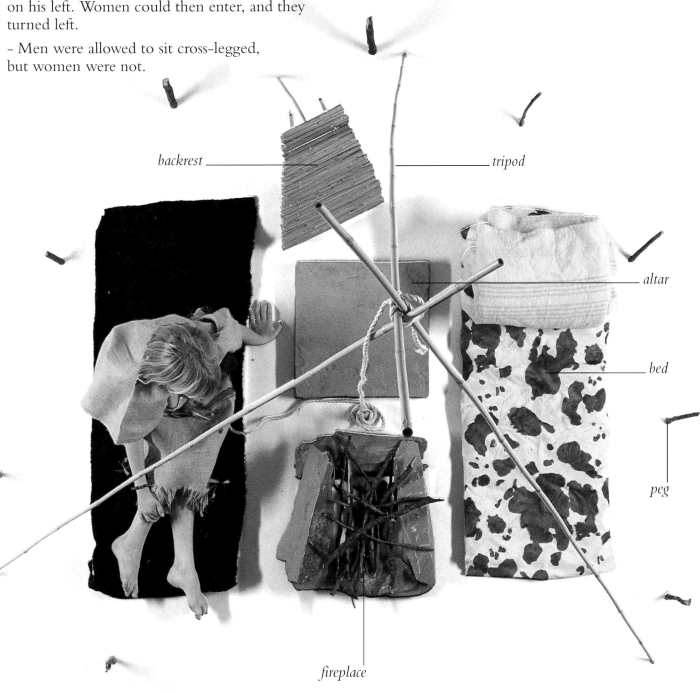

backrest

tripod

altar

bed

peg

fireplace

🏠 **THE IROQUOIS PEOPLES** settled on the east coast, in what is now southern Ontario, Quebec and New York State. They built villages and farmed the rich land, where there was plenty of firewood and clear, clean water from the many rivers and springs. They lived in close-knit groups and their villages were collections of enormous longhouses, surrounded by high, protective fences, or palisades, made of sharp stakes. But these villages were not really permanent. Early farming methods exhausted the land after about 20 years. When the crops would no longer grow, it was time to move on and rebuild in a more fertile place.

🏠 **LONGHOUSES** were as high as they were wide, and in some cases as long as a football field. One house was home to a group of related fireside families. Each family had its own space along the side of the house, and shared a fire in the central corridor with the family opposite. There was a door at each end, but no windows. Smoke from the fires eventually found its way out through a series of ventilation holes in the roof, but the inside was very smoky. As a result, many longhouse people suffered from eye trouble and became blind as they grew old.

🏠 MAKE A LONGHOUSE

fire corridor   *sleeping platform*

You will need: base board, three lengths of wood (two thick, one thin), thick and thin twigs, DIY filler, soil, glue, scraps of fabric or leather

1 Make sleeping platforms and a fire corridor by laying the strips of wood parallel to one another, with the thinner one in the middle.

2 Cut some thick twigs to the same length and glue them upright, spacing them equally on the board.

3 Mix the filler with water to make a paste and spread it over the board and platforms. Sprinkle the soil over the wet filler so that it sticks.

4 Cut beams from thick twigs to make the roof frame. Stick pairs of beams together to make the roof shape, as shown, and glue them in place on the top of each pair of upright posts. Make a framework of thin twigs over the walls and roof to form a support for the bark tiles.

5 Cut the fabric or leather roughly into squares. Glue them on to the framework in overlapping layers, starting at the bottom so that there are no cracks for rain to seep in. Glue a lattice of thin twigs over the top of the tiles.

6 Make a palisade from sharpened twigs. Stick them to the base board, sharp ends up and pointing outwards, to form a defensive wall around the longhouse.

▼ MAKE AN EARTH LODGE

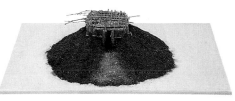

You will need: base board, thick and thin twigs, moss or leaves, soil, glue

1 Cut all the thick twigs to the same length and glue upright to the base board in a square. Leave a small gap in one side for the doorway.

2 Lay a lattice of thinner twigs over the top and cover with moss or leaves. Pile soil over the frame to form a cone, leaving a clear pathway to the door.

When Navajo people built their earth lodges, they hammered the frame posts into the ground, with each post touching the next, to form a solid wall of timber. They made the doorway the width of a man's shoulders, so the house was easier to defend against intruders.

bark tiles

upright beam

roof beam

framework of thin poles to hold tiles down in high winds

palisade to defend the longhouse village

🏠 **LONGHOUSE BUILDING MATERIALS** were mainly wood and bark. The outer frame was made from thick posts, firmly driven into the ground. Horizontal beams were lashed in place with strong bark fibres. The roof frame was made from thinner poles and the whole house was covered with overlapping tiles of ash or elm tree bark.

🏠 **THE PALISADE** was made from stakes which were spaced so that the distance between them was just the width of a man's shoulders. Villagers could come and go freely but attacking warriors had to thread their way through with their arms pinned to their sides, making it very difficult to use their weapons.

Tribes and families

A Plains Indian village was made up of groups of families, or **clans**, who often traced their relationship to one another through the women of the family. There could be 50 or more loosely-related clans in a tribe, which occupied an area of land, or territory. The most important ties were not to the tribe but to the immediate family. The mother, father and children who shared a home and a fireside are sometimes called a fireside family.

🔺 **TEPEES** were set up with their entrances facing east, to keep out the winds that usually blew across the open Plains from the west. They were grouped according to family relationships.

▽ *Tepee villages were built on carefully chosen sites, close to a river or stream and sheltered from the wind wherever possible.*

strips of buffalo meat curing in the sun

door flap

buffalo chips for making a fire

tepee frame

🔺 **LIFE ON THE MOVE** meant a tough routine for the Indians who hunted buffalo in the vast, dry, windy central Plains. They spent their lives packing up camp, dragging or carrying their possessions, and setting up camp all over again. But their efforts were repaid by a constant supply of food, clothing and shelter from the buffalo.

🔺 **VILLAGES** were run by chiefs and elders, who were chosen by their fellow villagers to offer wise advice, rather than to tell people what to do. Most people could do as they chose, as long as they worked for the general good. Men usually hunted and fought, while most women cleaned skins, made clothes, put up tepees and cooked.

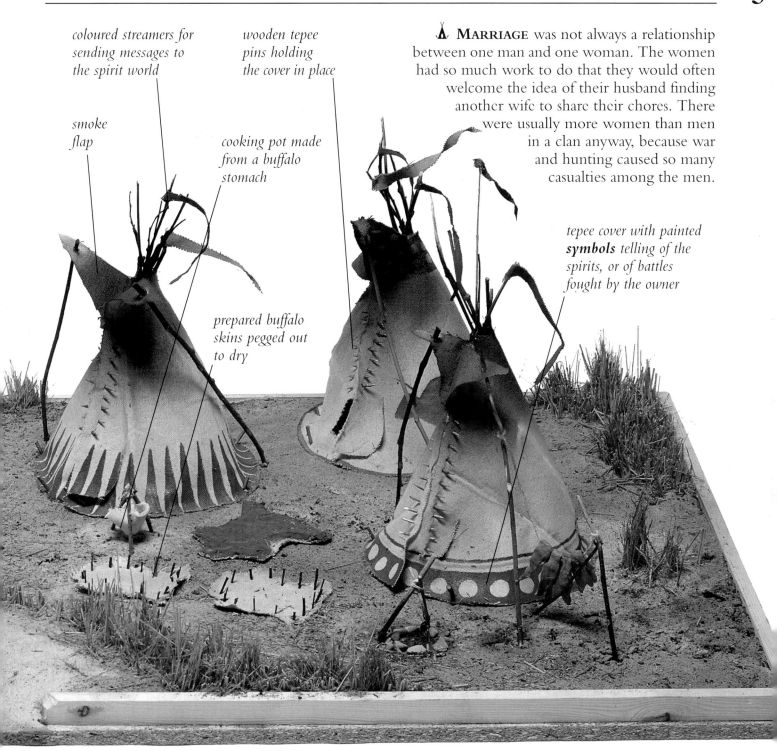

coloured streamers for
sending messages to
the spirit world

wooden tepee
pins holding
the cover in place

smoke
flap

cooking pot made
from a buffalo
stomach

prepared buffalo
skins pegged out
to dry

⚊ MARRIAGE was not always a relationship between one man and one woman. The women had so much work to do that they would often welcome the idea of their husband finding another wife to share their chores. There were usually more women than men in a clan anyway, because war and hunting caused so many casualties among the men.

tepee cover with painted
symbols telling of the
spirits, or of battles
fought by the owner

⚊ CHILDREN had a carefree time, playing with toy bows, tepees or dolls and learning about the life they would lead as adults. They were always expected to behave in a way that would bring no danger or dishonour to their clan or group. They learned very quickly not to cry or make a fuss if an enemy was near.

⚊ WARRIORS were usually men, but some women also fought and hunted. Men thought so highly of one Crow warrior woman, known as Woman Chief, that they were scared to ask to marry her. She 'married' four women so she would have someone to look after her tepee. If a man preferred to work in the home, no one minded.

♠ **THE NORTHWESTERN TRIBES** lived in fishing villages on the strip of land between the mountains and the sea. There were nearly 50 tribes there, leading well-ordered, comfortable lives. They had a flourishing trade in dried and smoked fish and finely woven basketware, making them the richest of the North American Indians. These were the tribes most concerned with showing their social rank and wealth.

♠ **WOODEN HOUSES** were strung out in villages along the coastline, with all the houses facing the sea. Each plank house was home to several related families and the carved **totem poles** outside let everyone know the histories of the families living there.

△ *Totem poles were made by skilled carvers of the Northwestern tribes. Their main function was to record family crests and glorious moments of family history.*

♠ MAKE A PLANK HOUSE AND TOTEM POLE

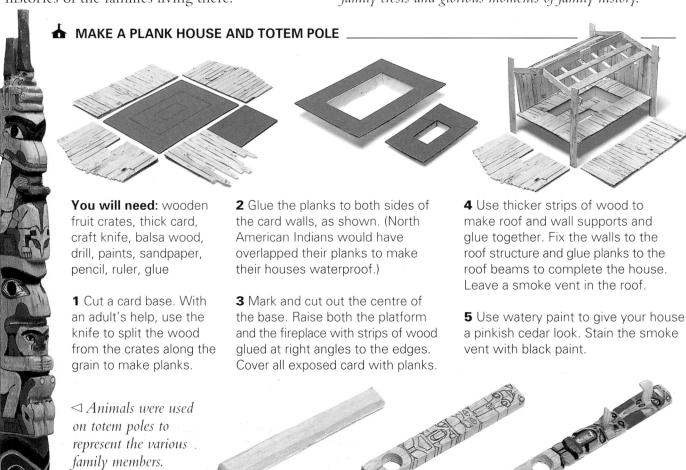

◁ *Animals were used on totem poles to represent the various family members.*

You will need: wooden fruit crates, thick card, craft knife, balsa wood, drill, paints, sandpaper, pencil, ruler, glue

1 Cut a card base. With an adult's help, use the knife to split the wood from the crates along the grain to make planks.

2 Glue the planks to both sides of the card walls, as shown. (North American Indians would have overlapped their planks to make their houses waterproof.)

3 Mark and cut out the centre of the base. Raise both the platform and the fireplace with strips of wood glued at right angles to the edges. Cover all exposed card with planks.

4 Use thicker strips of wood to make roof and wall supports and glue together. Fix the walls to the roof structure and glue planks to the roof beams to complete the house. Leave a smoke vent in the roof.

5 Use watery paint to give your house a pinkish cedar look. Stain the smoke vent with black paint.

6 To make a totem pole, cut a piece of balsa wood a little taller than your house. Sand it to make a flattened cylinder shape and drill a hole for the doorway as shown.

7 Draw out your design and carve the lines with a craft knife. Glue on extra pieces for wings or beaks. Sand and paint your totem pole and glue to the front of your plank house.

⌂ CEDAR WOOD was easy to carve and hollow out to make **canoes**. The stringy bark gave fibre for making baskets, ropes and clothes. Northwestern Indians believed that these trees must be on Earth to help humans.

⌂ RAINFALL is high on the Northwest Coast, and the winters are cold. Plank houses were made of overlapping cedar planks so that the rain ran off. They had no windows, just a hole in the roof which could be closed with a wooden shutter.

⌂ A PLANK HOUSE was home for up to six families, related through the women. Their shared living space was about 15 metres square, with a sunken area in the centre where children played and women cooked. A sleeping platform around the edge was divided into family spaces, with the most important family at the back and the lowliest near the draughty door.

⌂ A POTLATCH was organized by a Northwestern family to celebrate a special event, such as a wedding. They put on a lavish feast and gave their guests many valuable gifts, including canoes, slaves, furs and blankets. The more gifts a host gave, the higher his status rose. The guests who received the most then had to throw an even greater potlatch. Among Northwestern tribes, being wealthy meant being more important. People used potlatches to show how rich they were, and to settle old rivalries. Through potlatching, they could force their rivals to give away everything they owned.

smoke hole in roof

totem pole

A healthy diet

North American Indians lived on a healthy diet of meat or fish, grain, nuts, fruit and other food plants. Most tribes had learned how to preserve meat and fish by drying or smoking, so there were always emergency supplies if the hunters came back empty-handed.

⚑ ANIMALS that provided food for the Indians were treated with great respect. A ceremony was held for the first salmon caught in each run. It was taken to a special altar, welcomed with speeches and cooked with great care. They believed that there were people living in the sea who took the form of salmon each year. If they were not treated properly, they might never come again.

⚑ BUFFALO HUNTING was exhausting and lonely, but was seen as very noble. A hunter would spend most of his time tracking and killing buffalo, a dangerous task done on foot before Europeans brought horses to North America. To succeed, men had to be in tune with nature and the animals they hunted. They sometimes dressed in a buffalo skin and moved amongst the herd. They only took what they needed and never killed just for the sake of it.

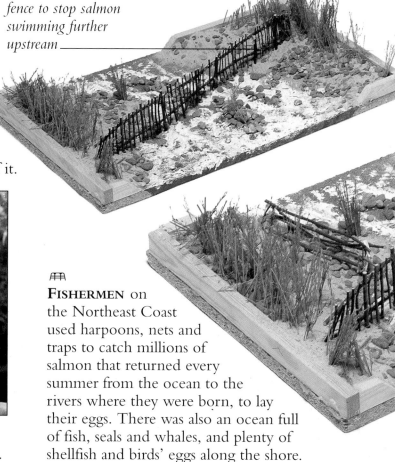

fence to stop salmon swimming further upstream

△ *Ishi, a Californian Yahi Indian, photographed in 1914 making a leister, a harpoon for spearing salmon.*

⚑ FISHERMEN on the Northeast Coast used harpoons, nets and traps to catch millions of salmon that returned every summer from the ocean to the rivers where they were born, to lay their eggs. There was also an ocean full of fish, seals and whales, and plenty of shellfish and birds' eggs along the shore.

⚑ MAKE A SALMON TRAP

You will need: base board, paint, dried grasses, stones, twigs, sand, craft knife, glue

1 Paint a river on the board. Make sand banks either side, dotted with dried grasses and pebbles.

2 Build a fence across the river. Glue the crosspieces to the supports.

(Northeastern Indians would have pushed the supports into the ground and tied the sticks with sinew.)

The fence stops the salmon from swimming further upstream. As they will never turn back, they struggle and leap against the fence, while more fish keep coming up behind them.

3 Make trapping gates in the same way as the fence. Bend twigs to make the rounded ends of the tunnel-shaped pens. Add to the fence.

Men with spears would have waded into the killing pen. Any fish not harpooned at once were swept back by the current into the trapping gates and collected in the pens.

⊞ **PREPARING AND PRESERVING FISH** was done by the women. The rich fish oil was highly prized and used as grease for cooking and for lamps. It was traded along 'grease trails' down the coast and over the mountains.

▷ *Fish traps were made to much the same design all over the Northeast and Subarctic.*

killing pen

trapping gate

tunnel-shaped pen

SOUTHEASTERN HUNTERS caught small animals in traps. They used blowpipes and poison darts to hunt deer. Some could knock birds from the sky with a **bola**, made from a stone tied to a line of sinew, which they whirled around their heads before letting it fly.

THE THREE MAIN FOOD CROPS grown by North American Indians were corn, beans and squash. Farmers used tools made of wood or bone. Men turned the earth and women planted the seeds.

RUBBING STICKS TOGETHER to make fire took so long that fires were often left smouldering all day. Many huntsmen travelled with a slow-burning rope so they had a quick way of lighting fire when they set up camp.

RICH SOIL meant good crops, and Indian farmers believed in putting something back into the earth in thanks for what came out. The Iroquois, for example, put herrings into the ground before they sowed corn. The goodness in the fish made the soil much richer.

A TYPICAL IROQUOIS MEAL included roasted meat, raw salad, baked pumpkin and corn dumplings. Families ate just once a day, before noon. Meals were eaten in silence, standing or squatting on the ground. Men ate first, and women and children ate what was left. Children were told that if they did not thank their parents for each meal, they would be punished with a stomach ache.

▼ MAKE HOPI BOILED CORN CAKES

You will need: 3 cornhusks (the outer part of a corn cob), 1 cup of cornmeal flour, half a cup of honey, blue food colouring (optional)

1 Boil the cornhusks until they are soft. Drain them and let them cool.

2 Put the cornmeal in a bowl and gradually add about a cup of boiling water, until the mixture is like thick custard.

3 Stir the honey into the mixture and add blue colouring if you like. (The Hopi grew blue corn, so their corn cakes had a bluish tinge.)

4 Open out the cornhusks and drop 2 spoonfuls of corn mixture into the centre of about 20 of them. Fold them neatly into parcels. Shred the remaining husks and use the shreds to tie up the parcels.

5 Ask an adult to help you bring water to the boil in a large saucepan, then carefully put in the corn cake parcels.

6 Boil the parcels for 15 to 20 minutes, then take them out with a slotted spoon. Let them cool before you unwrap and eat them.

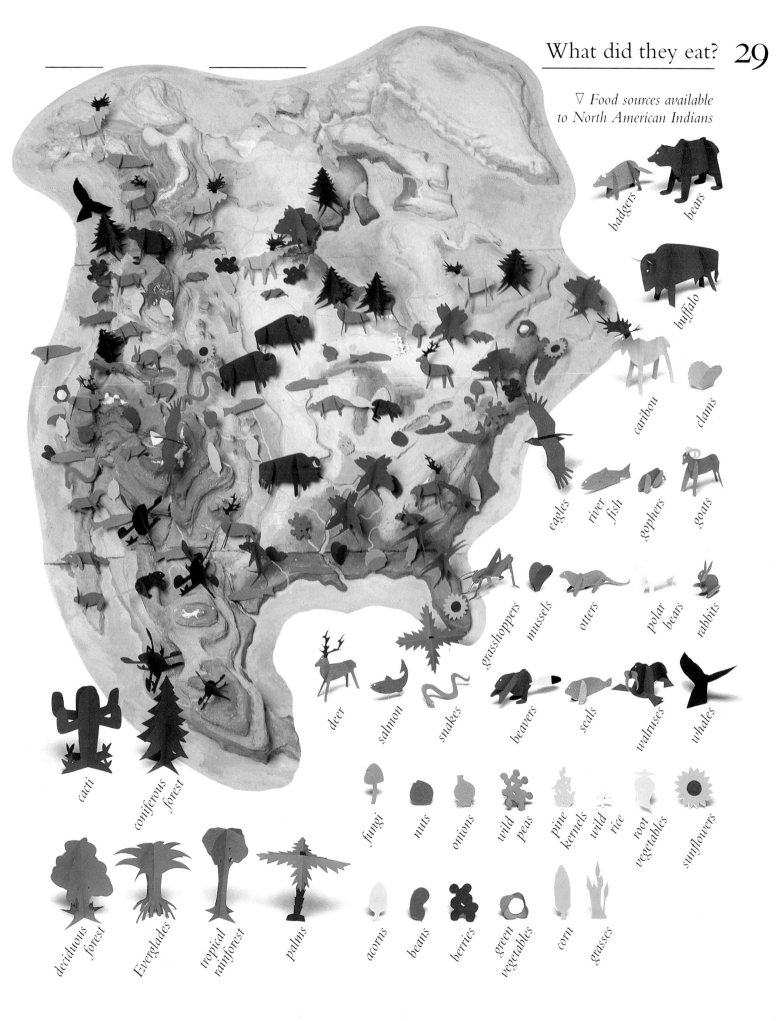

▽ *Food sources available to North American Indians*

badgers

bears

buffalo

caribou

clams

eagles

river fish

gophers

goats

grasshoppers

mussels

otters

polar bears

rabbits

deer

salmon

snakes

beavers

seals

walruses

whales

cacti

coniferous forest

fungi

nuts

onions

wild peas

pine kernels

wild rice

root vegetables

sunflowers

deciduous forest

Everglades

tropical rainforest

palms

acorns

beans

berries

green vegetables

corn

grasses

Sport and leisure

Most North American Indian games and sports were a preparation for life. Men played vigorous team games to help prepare themselves for war, and hunting games to sharpen their skills. Women played games of skill and chance, using their everyday work tools. Both men and women also liked to sing as they placed bets in games of chance. They made music to summon up good spirits and good luck.

△ *Lacrosse* players were allowed two sticks each.

MAKE A LACROSSE STICK

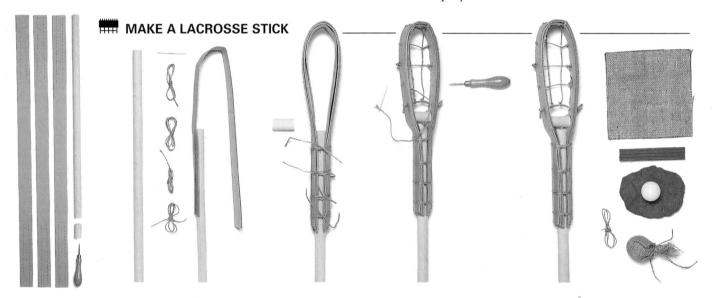

You will need: broomstick or thick dowelling, strong card, string, glue, bradawl, saw, ping-pong ball, square of sacking or other fabric, Plasticine

1 Ask an adult to help you cut three strips of card, and to cut the handle and spacer bar from the dowelling. Bend one strip of card around and carefully glue both ends to the handle, as shown.

2 Repeat with the other two strips, until you have a loop made of three thicknesses of card. (The North American Indians would have used strips of hide.) Use string to tie the loop securely in place.

3 Push in the spacer bar at the top of the handle and glue it into place. Use the bradawl very carefully to make holes around the loop.

4 Thread string through the holes to make the net, as shown. Knot the ends on the outside of the loop to hold the net in place.

5 To make the ball, flatten the Plasticine and wrap it tightly around the ping-pong ball. Cover with the square of fabric and tie tightly with string. (North American Indians used a ball of animal hair, covered with hide.)

GAMBLING GAMES were very popular with women, who sometimes played for very high stakes, such as offering to become a slave to the other player. Games were more often played for furs, skins, household goods, moccasins or horses.

POST BALL

POST BALL was played just for fun by both men and women. They set up a post in the village square and the object was to hit the post with a ball. The women could use their hands, but the men could use only sticks.

throwing the ball

picking up the ball

tackling, or checking, to get the ball from another player's net

players jumping to catch the ball in their nets

WAR'S LITTLE BROTHER was a fearsome game. It is still played today in a much more controlled form, known as lacrosse. Then, up to 100 people could play in each team. The pitch had no boundaries and the huge goals could be up to 100 metres wide. Players had to hurl a ball through the goal posts, and the game was won by the first team to score 12 goals. It often lasted for hours. There were no rules of fair play so it was a bloody battle, with many casualties. Players were pushed, beaten with sticks, often badly injured and sometimes killed.

THE AWL GAME was a game of chance. The board was marked out on a blanket. Each player pinned an awl (a tool used for piercing hides) through the blanket in various places. They moved their awls around the blanket in opposite directions.

FOUR STICKS were thrown at the central stone to decide each move. One carried a special mark. If a stick fell flat side up, it counted for one move. If the mark came up, it meant an extra throw. The board showed dry and flowing rivers. Dry rivers were safe, but players who fell in flowing rivers or on an opponent's position had to go back to the start.

MUSIC AND DANCE were central to the Indian way of life and everybody took part. People believed that music was the language of the spirits. Mothers sang lullabies to their children, warriors sang to call upon their guardian spirits, hunters made magic animal music and farmers chanted to their crops. There were ceremonial songs for births, marriages, deaths and funerals.

▷ *These Ute musicians and dancers in the Great Basin and Plateau area were photographed in 1900.*

RATTLES, RASPS AND DRUMS were used to create rhythms. Turtle shells, coconuts, gourds, and buffalo horns were natural percussion instruments. People made other instruments from wood or hide. A gourd rattle's sound could be improved by putting pebbles or beans inside, along with a few of the original seeds to help the rattle keep its spiritual powers.

rattle

🛖 MAKE A RATTLE

You will need: a tennis ball, dried beans or peas, dowelling, glue, paper, paint, thick string, coloured raffia

1 Make holes on either side of the tennis ball, put the beans inside and push the dowelling through, as shown.

2 Tear the paper into pieces and glue them on to the ball in a smooth papier-mâché layer. When the glue has dried, wind the string round the handle and ball, sticking it in place as you go. Leave a gap around the middle of the ball.

3 Decorate the rattle by painting a pattern on the plain part of the ball and adding a raffia tail.

⚠ MAKE A DRUM AND DRUM STICK

You will need: a flower pot, canvas or other fabric, glue, thin string, paints, felt-tip pens, two thin sticks or dowels, Plasticine, string, raffia

1 Cut a curved piece of fabric to fit around the pot and glue it on. Cut another piece to fit over the top and reach well down the sides.

2 Plait the string to make a decorative cord. Stretch the fabric over the pot and use the cord to tie it firmly in place just below the rim.

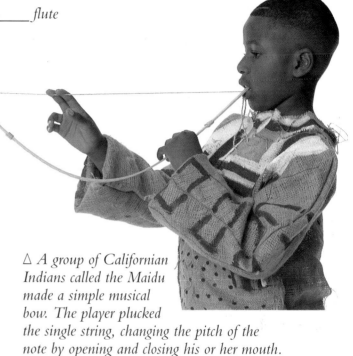

flute

FLUTES were carved from soft wood, which was split in half, hollowed out and stuck together with glue made from boiled hide scrapings and bound with rawhide strips. They were used for playing love songs. The Sioux called their courting whistles 'moose whistles' after the sound made by a bull moose in the mating season.

WHISTLES made music for war. Warriors rode into battle blowing whistles made from eagle bones. Eagles were a symbol for courage.

INDIAN SONGS were not complicated. They had a simple tune, usually going down the scale from high notes to low notes. Songs and chants were owned by the person who had made them up. If the singer had enjoyed a long and happy life, the right to sing the song would be passed on to their family or even sold for a high price.

△ *A group of Californian Indians called the Maidu made a simple musical bow. The player plucked the single string, changing the pitch of the note by opening and closing his or her mouth.*

THROBBING DRUMS were like a heartbeat to the Indians. Their sound was sacred, particularly that of the water drum, which could only be played by those thought worthy, such as distinguished warriors.

4 Stick blobs of Plasticine to the end of each stick and cover with fabric tied with string. Decorate with raffia and paint patterns on the sticks.

3 Finish off with a loop of cord for a handle. Paint the drum to make the cloth look like buffalo hide. Wetting the fabric with paint will shrink it and improve the tone of the drum. Use felt-tips to decorate the drum.

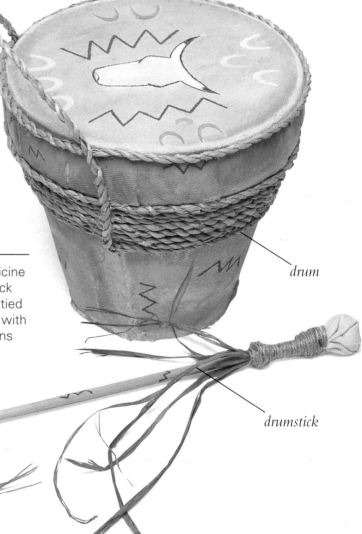

drum

drumstick

Arts and crafts

In some **cultures**, art is a way of showing things as they are. For North American Indians, art was more than that. It was a way of expressing their hopes and fears, of thanking the Creator for nature's gifts and pleasing the Creator with prayers and promises. Because of this, their art was symbolic. They used symbols and signs to represent their ideas, beliefs, dreams and visions. When Indian artists drew an animal or person, they were trying to show the inner spirit, not the outer appearance.

△ *This Californian Karok basket-maker was photographed in 1896. She is using the twining method, rather than the coiling technique shown below.*

🔺 **BASKETS** were made by almost all Indians, but the tribes of the Southwest were particularly skilful basket-weavers. They used them for everything from cradles, storage chests and sieves to bird and fish traps, backpacks, hats and mats. Some were so tightly woven that they were waterproof, and could even be used for brewing beer. Materials included rushes, bear grass, yucca leaves and willow, steamed until the fibres were supple. Symbolic designs were woven into the baskets using fibres that had been coloured with mineral or vegetable dyes.

(•) MAKE A BASKET

You will need: thick twine or plaited string, raffia, darning needle

1 Thread the needle with a length of raffia. You will need several lengths to make the basket.

2 Begin the basket base by coiling the twine or plaited string tightly. Work outwards from the centre. Sew each layer to the last one, as you build up the coils.

3 Once you have a flat base, about five coils deep, begin to build up the sides of the basket. Finish off by sewing down the end of the twine securely.

▷ *These Pueblo pots were used for storage, cooking and eating.*

POT-MAKING was a skill that probably came from the Mexico area, where there was plenty of clay in the soil. In some places, such as parts of California, pots were not made at all because clay was hard to find and baskets served every possible need.

🔊 **FIRING POTS** to turn soft mud into hard pottery was done by baking them at a high temperature for a long time. They were buried in a mound of dried animal dung, which burnt more evenly than wood.

🔊 **MAKE A CLAY POT**

You will need: self-hardening clay, pencil, paint

1 Flatten and pinch out a clay base as shown.

2 Roll the clay into thin sausages, and begin to build up the sides of the pot by coiling the clay around. Make the pot wider as it grows taller, then narrower at the neck. (Southwestern tribes used coiling for making pots, and they used the same technique for baskets.)

3 Smooth the outside of the pot, allow it to dry and then draw and paint your design. (The Indians stamped symbolic patterns on soft clay or scraped designs on hardened clay. They coloured pots white, brown, red and yellow, using pigments from the earth.)

TEXTILES have been woven in North America for 2,000 years. Very early cloth was not woven on a loom. The threads were made by spinning fibres from plants and animal hair, and woven together by knitting, crochet, plaiting and twining in many different ways.

THE DYES AND PAINTS used by North American Indians were made from minerals and plants. Minerals are found in different coloured soils. Iron in soil gives a range of reds, yellows and browns. Soil with copper makes greens and blues. Graphite makes black, and clay, limestone and gypsum make white. Colour can also be taken from plants, berries, roots, moss and bark. Boiling or soaking the materials with the plant changes their colour.

DESIGNS AND COLOURS had different meanings for different tribes, and even for individual artists. Sometimes the artist had a dream that showed him or her what designs and colours to use. Although it is difficult to say exactly what particular colours meant, there were some general uses:

Blue	Female, moon, sky, water, thunder, sadness
Black	Male, cold, night, disease, death, underworld
Green	Earth, summer, rain, plants
Red	War, day, blood, wounds, sunset
White	Winter, death, snow
Yellow	Day, dawn, sunshine

DYEING FABRIC

 turmeric makes bright yellow

 onion skin makes yellowy brown

 blueberries make mauve

 avocado pear skin makes pink

You will need: white cotton fabric, piece of muslin, string, ingredients for colour (see left), cutting board, knife, old pan, wooden spoon, jug or bowl, strainer

1 Choose which colours you want to dye your fabric and prepare the ingredients. Place them on the muslin and tie into a bundle with the string.

2 Put the fabric and muslin bundle into the pan. Cover with water and ask an adult to help you boil it.

3 When the fabric has changed colour, let the dye cool and strain it into the jug so you can re-use it.

4 Let the fabric dry out naturally. Remember that the colour will fade and run if you wash it.

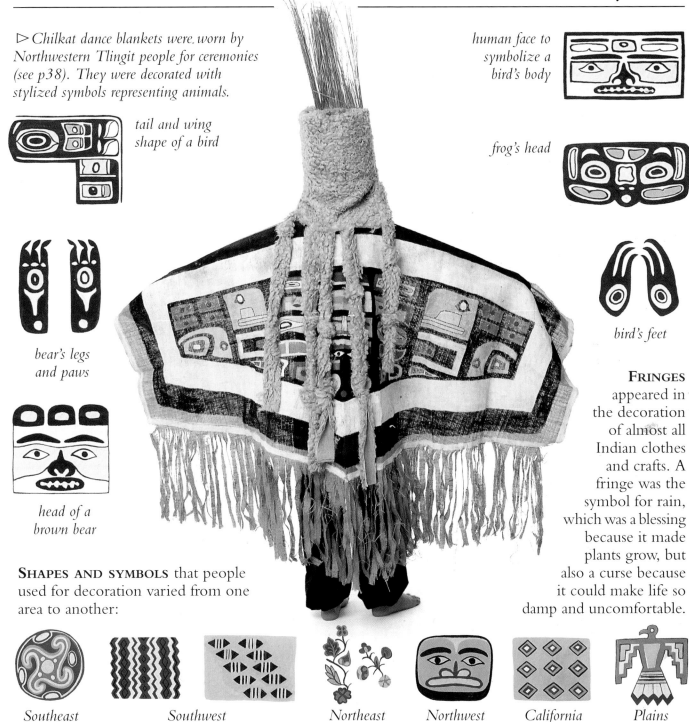

▷ *Chilkat dance blankets were worn by Northwestern Tlingit people for ceremonies (see p38). They were decorated with stylized symbols representing animals.*

tail and wing shape of a bird

human face to symbolize a bird's body

frog's head

bear's legs and paws

bird's feet

head of a brown bear

FRINGES appeared in the decoration of almost all Indian clothes and crafts. A fringe was the symbol for rain, which was a blessing because it made plants grow, but also a curse because it could make life so damp and uncomfortable.

SHAPES AND SYMBOLS that people used for decoration varied from one area to another:

Southeast   *Southwest*   *Northeast*   *Northwest*   *California*   *Plains*

CURVES AND SPIRALS were popular in the Southeast, where bird and animal shapes were often used.

PARALLEL LINES as well as curves feature in the culture of the Southwest.

THE FLOWING LINES of plant and flower shapes were used by woodlanders in the Northeast.

BIRDS, FISH AND HUMAN FACES featured in the Northwest, often within a curved shape.

TRIANGLES, RECTANGLES AND SQUARES were used in many designs in California, especially for basket work.

GEOMETRIC SHAPES, particularly triangles, were popular with the Plains Indians.

SIMPLE LOOMS with a fixed warp (the vertical threads) were used in ancient times in the Southwest. Later, people in this area developed the true loom. It had a pair of horizontal sticks separating every other thread of the warp. The weft (the horizontal threads) could then be pushed through from side to side with a shuttle, making weaving much easier and quicker.

THE CHILKAT, a branch of the Tlingit tribe, were expert weavers. In their homelands, there were no flocks of fleecy sheep and no wild cotton, just mountains and cedar trees. People wove with the hair of wild mountain goats and shredded fibres from the soft inner bark of cedar trees. A blanket took up to a year to make.

MAKE A SIMPLE WEAVING FRAME

You will need: strips of wood, glue, pencil, ruler, small nails, hammer, large bodkin, coloured wool

1 Glue and nail the strips of wood to make the frame, as shown. Measure and mark positions for the nails at each end. Make them close together and evenly spaced. Ask an adult to help you hammer the nails in.

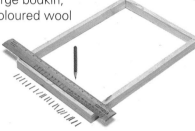

2 To make the warp, tie a piece of wool to the first nail at one corner. Stretch it back and forth across the frame, looping it around the nails. Tie it off on the last nail.

3 To make the weft, thread a length of coloured wool through the bodkin and wind it around as shown.

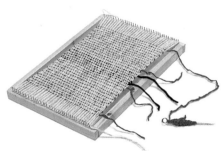

4 Tie the loose end of the wool to the outside warp thread, then weave the bodkin in and out from side to side.

5 When you want to change colour, tie the new wool to the outside warp thread as before.

6 When you have filled the frame, tie the end of your last weft row to the outside warp thread and carefully lift your finished piece off the nails. Tie together the two loops at each corner.

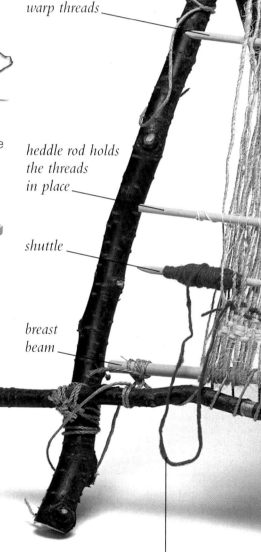

shed rod makes the shed, or space, between the warp threads

heddle rod holds the threads in place

shuttle

breast beam

weft or horizontal thread

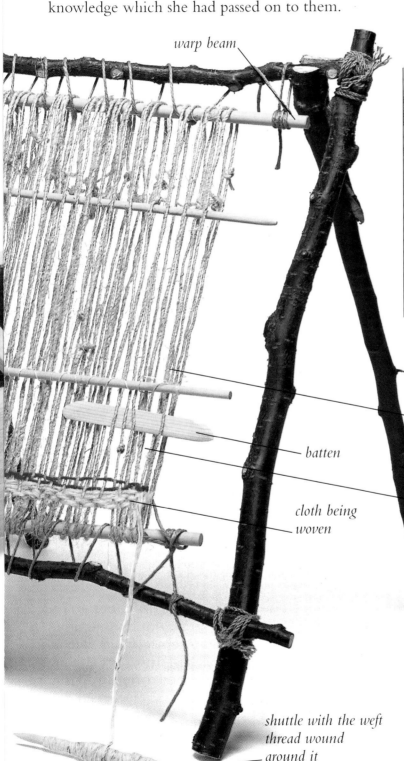

⛏ **THE SPIDERWOMAN** was a spirit who wove webs to catch rain clouds, and had taught the first people on Earth how to weave. Weavers in the Southwest used the symbol of the spiderwoman in their designs as a way of thanking her for the knowledge which she had passed on to them.

warp beam

△ Present-day Navajo Indians weave using the traditional methods and designs.

warp or vertical thread

batten

weaving frame

shed, or space where the shuttle passes through

cloth being woven

shuttle with the weft thread wound around it

⛏ **THE NAVAJO** are perhaps best known for their beautifully woven blankets with strong, geometric designs. The ideas for the designs, it is said, came directly from the weaver's inner spirit. The women who made them boasted that their blankets were so closely woven, they could hold water. They always made a tiny mistake in the weaving, as they believed if they were ever to make one perfect thing, their lives would be complete and their time on Earth would be over.

BOATS OF DIFFERENT SHAPES
were built for different conditions.
Tribes living by lakes and riversides
needed light, easy-to-steer canoes
that they could take out of the
water and carry when it became
too dangerous or shallow. Small
canoes were perfect for shooting over
waterfalls, but larger boats were needed
for carrying goods for trading. A boat with
a low bow and stern is good in calm waters.
A high bow and stern give protection from
rough waters but slow the boat down because
of greater wind resistance.

gunwale   *decorative stitching*

wooden paddle

BIRCH TREES were plentiful in the Northeast
and the Great Lakes area. These tall, thin, straight
trees are wrapped in up to nine layers of bark
which come off in sheets when carefully
peeled. The outer skin is thick and
white, the inner skins thinner,
browner and softer.

CANOE BARK was peeled from a cut
tree in the spring, when the outer layer is at its
thickest. It was used, brown side out and white
side in, to cover a frame of cedar wood. The
bark sheets were sewn together with spruce
roots. The seams were then made waterproof
with a covering of gummy sap from the pine
tree, heated until it became
a thick, gooey syrup.

PADDLES were shaped from wood,
anchors made from stones, bailers from
shells and ropes from plant fibre or strips
of hide. North American Indians saw no
need for sails on their boats. They did not
particularly want to go where the wind blew
them, so paddles were all they needed for their
short fishing and trading trips.

MAKE A BIRCH BARK CANOE

You will need: thick and thin balsa
wood strips, bulldog clips, craft knife,
pencil, needle, thread, paints, glue

1 Take the thick strip of balsa, mark
out the gunwale (the top part) of the
canoe as shown, and cut it out
carefully, using a craft knife.

2 Soak the thin strips of balsa in
hot water for half an hour. Lay the
gunwale over the strips and fold
them upwards to make the sides
of the canoe. Lift the gunwale into
position and glue it to the top of the
sides, using clips to hold it in place.

3 When dry, cut off any balsa
sticking out above the gunwale.
Glue on a thin finishing strip and
sew it in place as shown.

4 Sew thin strips of balsa wood
together to make ends of the canoe.

🏛 **BIRCH BARK CANOES** were light, portable boats made of bark stretched over a frame of saplings. They were used by the Algonquian peoples who lived, hunted and fished on the wooded shores and winding waterways around the Great Lakes. The design of their canoe remains practically unchanged. It came in two versions, a low-ended one for the rivers and a high-ended one for rougher waters.

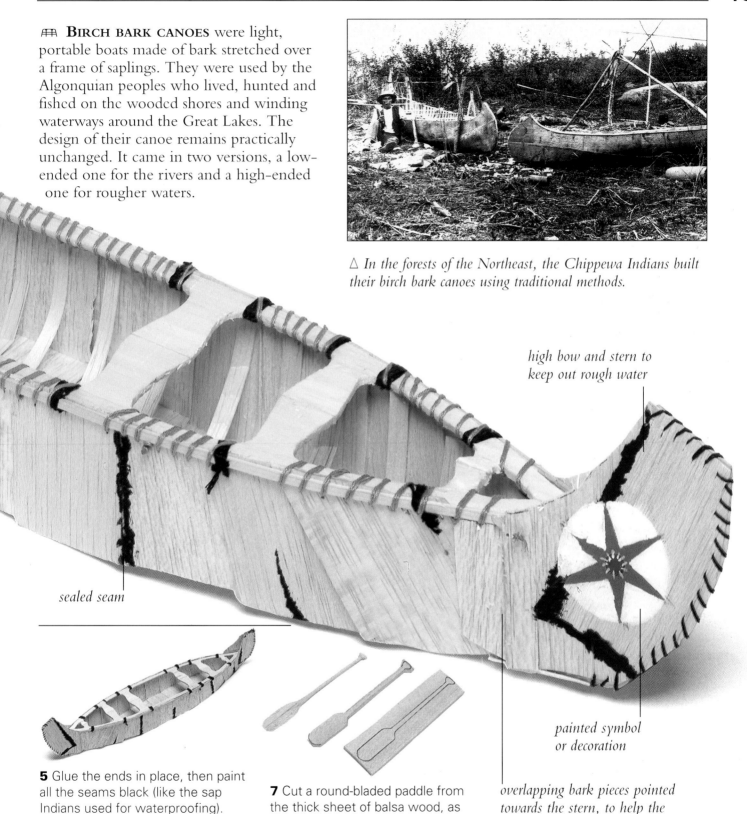

△ *In the forests of the Northeast, the Chippewa Indians built their birch bark canoes using traditional methods.*

high bow and stern to keep out rough water

sealed seam

painted symbol or decoration

overlapping bark pieces pointed towards the stern, to help the water flow easily around the canoe

5 Glue the ends in place, then paint all the seams black (like the sap Indians used for waterproofing).

6 Put thin reinforcing strips inside the canoe as shown. Decorate the canoe with stitching and motifs.

7 Cut a round-bladed paddle from the thick sheet of balsa wood, as shown. These paddles were designed for shooting rapids, because a rounded end is less likely to be damaged by stones and rocks.

🔺 **BEFORE THE HORSE** was introduced to North America about 400 years ago, all land journeys were made on foot. Anything that needed to be carried was hauled along by women, or by dogs pulling a **travois** made from two dragging poles attached to a harness. Nomadic Indians following a buffalo herd on foot covered only about ten kilometres a day. They had few possessions, and kept their tepees small so they were easy to carry.

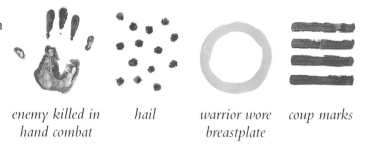

enemy killed in hand combat   *hail*   *warrior wore breastplate*   *coup marks*

△ *Plains warriors decorated their horses with painted symbols.*

🔺 **MAKE A TRAVOIS**

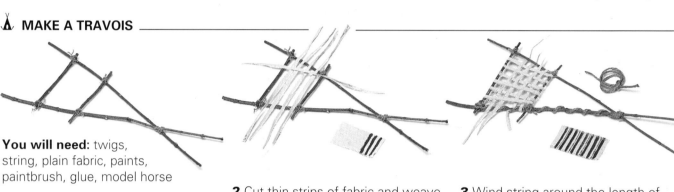

You will need: twigs, string, plain fabric, paints, paintbrush, glue, model horse

1 Use two long twigs and two short cross-pieces to make the basic shape, as shown. Tie them securely.

2 Cut thin strips of fabric and weave them to make a carrying platform. Glue to the frame. (Indians tied a travois with strips of buffalo hide.)

3 Wind string around the length of the poles and glue it. (Plains Indians used strips of hide for this, to protect the horse's skin from chafing.)

4 Bend and glue thin twigs to form a cage on the platform. Cut and paint a piece of fabric for the horse blanket. Paint symbols on the horse. Tie the poles and blanket to its back.

🔺 **AFTER THE HORSE** was brought to the **New World** by Spanish settlers, life for Plains Indians was transformed. They used horses to move swiftly in battle, to outrun buffalo and to pull the travois. A camp could now move 50 kilometres in one day. Tepees became bigger and more spacious. Women no longer had to carry heavy loads, and had more time for leisure and for making things. People owned more and could transport things more easily.

🔺 **A SIOUX SONG** tells of the respect and honour with which Plains warriors treated their horses:
My horse be swift in flight
Even like a bird:
My horse be swift in flight.
Bear me now in safety
Far from the enemy's arrows
And you shall be rewarded
With streamers and ribbons red.

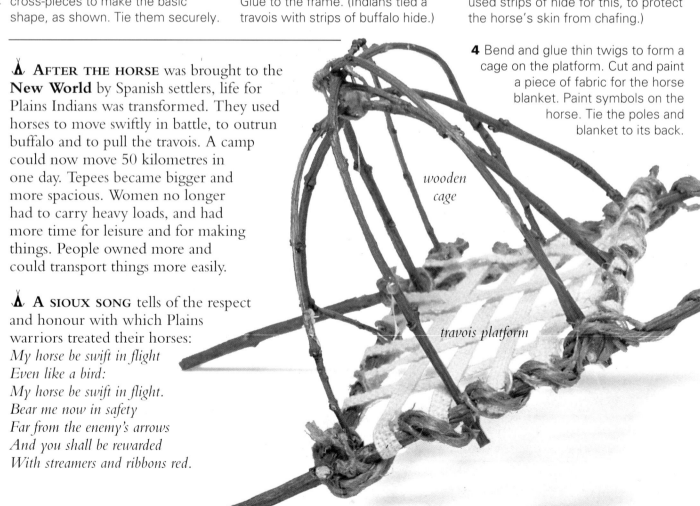

wooden cage

travois platform

△ *Young children often rode on a travois. Sometimes a wooden cage was put over the platform to keep passengers and possessions from falling off.*

⚐ SADDLES AND BRIDLES were made from buffalo hide and hair. A braided buffalo-hair rope or a thin strip of rawhide looped around the horse's lower jaw was all Plains horsemen needed to control their horses. While out hunting or fighting they rode bareback or used a simple hide saddle stuffed with buffalo hair. Women had wooden saddles padded with hide. Stirrups were made from wood, steamed into shape and covered in rawhide. Wealthy horse owners often had their tack decorated with paint and beads.

⚐ TRAVOIS were made by women. They were proud of their craftsmanship and were thought to be bad wives if their hide straps were cut unevenly or, worse still, had hair on them.

⚐ BABIES were carried on cradleboards by their mothers. They were tightly wrapped up and strapped on with leather thongs, so that they could not wriggle about and were kept warm and safe.

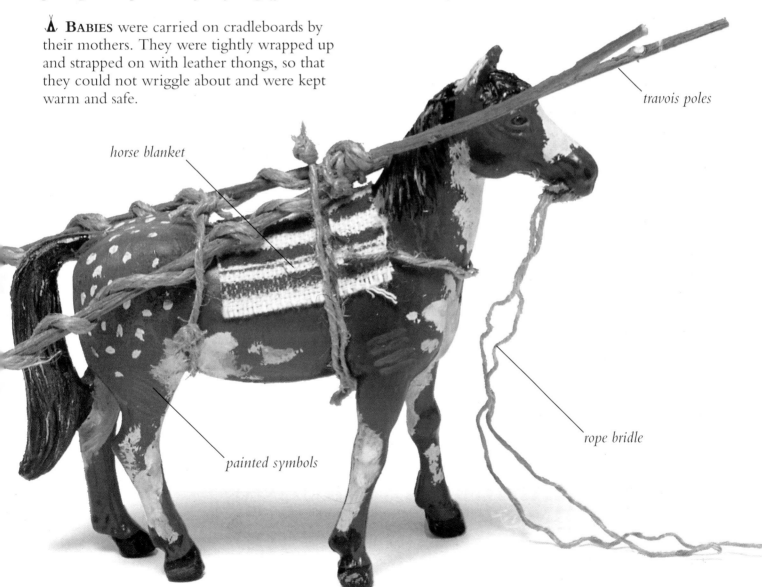

travois poles

horse blanket

rope bridle

painted symbols

Why make war?

war club

It started with the hunt. A hunter needed to be brave, confident and skilful, and was rewarded with glory and praise if he was successful. For North American Indians, the respect given to successful hunters was perhaps the most important thing in life. War was seen as the greatest hunt of all, offering men the chance to come home heroes. Raids for horses and arguments over hunting grounds were among the many reasons why they set out on the warpath.

△ *This Plains warrior was an Arapaho chief in 1870.*

INDIAN WARRIORS crept up on the enemy quickly and quietly, attacked fiercely, then turned and ran for it. There was no shame in retreat.

coup stick

BRAVERY was measured by how close warriors got to their enemy. Riding in close to touch the enemy with a coup stick was called counting coup. It was seen as more courageous than killing at 50 metres with a bow and arrow.

A BOW WITH ARROWS was an Indian warrior's main weapon. The Sioux made their bows from ash wood, with a bow string made of two twisted sinews. A war bow could be fired more quickly than a gun and be deadly accurate over 100 metres.

MAKE A BOW AND ARROW

You will need: thin strip of wood, string, feather, piece of foam sponge, cotton thread, kebab stick, glue, paints, craft knife

1 Mark the bow as shown and shape and nick the ends as shown, using the craft knife carefully.

2 Make a loop in the string, thread into the nick at one end and tie to the other end, bending the bow a little as shown.

3 Wrap and glue two lengths of string around the bow to make a handgrip as shown.

4 Make flights for the arrow by splitting the spine of the feather and cutting out 3 small sections as shown above.

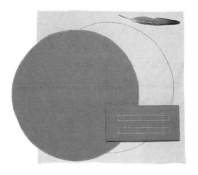
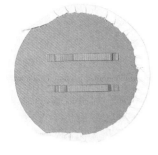

You will need: strong card, plain fabric, feathers, raffia, paint, pencil, bradawl

1 Cut a large card circle and a slightly larger fabric circle. Glue the fabric to the card, sticking it down around the edge, as shown. Cut two card strips as handles and glue to the back of the shield.

2 Draw your design on the front of the shield and paint it. Make small holes in the shield with the bradawl, thread raffia through them and tie on feathers as decoration.

⚲ **RAWHIDE SHIELDS** were painted with magic signs and kept wrapped up before battle so the magic could not leak away.

war axe

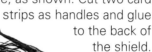

▦ **TOMAHAWKS** were curved, weighted clubs used for hitting enemies. They could also be thrown with fearsome force and accuracy.

spear

▦ **A CHEROKEE WARRIOR** said:
"We cannot live without war. Should we make peace with our present enemy, we must at once look out for some other people with whom we can indulge in our beloved occupation."

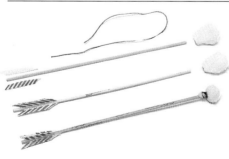

6 Paint and decorate both the bow and the arrow. Indian warriors painted pictures of their enemies on their arrows, so the arrows would know where to go. You can dip the arrow tips into paint and fire them at a target.

5 Glue the flights onto the kebab stick as shown. Cut the arrow down to half the length of the bow. Stick a small ball of foam onto the cut end of the arrow and secure with thread.

NEVER FIRE AN ARROW AT ANYONE. EVEN A TOY ARROW CAN CAUSE AN ACCIDENT.

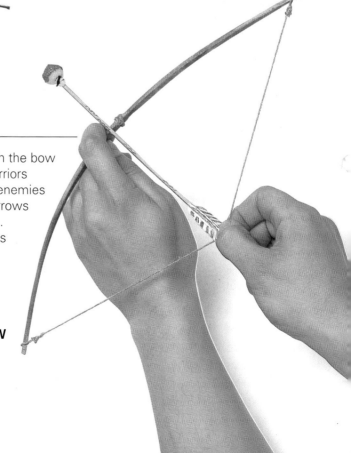

Language differences

As recently as 200 years ago, there were over 300 languages spoken in North America. None of these had any links to languages that were spoken in the **Old World**. Groups belonging to the same tribe did not necessarily speak the same language, and people who did share a language were often spread over a wide area, because of trade and nomadic ways of life. So Indians developed sign language to help them communicate with their neighbours. It allowed them to express emotions and feelings, as well as warnings and signals.

SIGN LANGUAGE used by North American Indians was made up of a mixture of mime and signalling, based on actions and shapes of things rather than on sounds. When Plains Indians visited Europe in the last century, they found they could communicate easily and naturally with deaf people.

EARLY EUROPEAN EXPLORERS and settlers tried to write down the sounds of Indian words, but some just could not be accurately conveyed using our alphabet. Some Indian words have turned into familiar place names:

Place	Pronunciation	Meaning
Alabama	alba-amo	plant reapers
Dakota	dak-hota	the friendly ones
Canada	kanata	cabin
Illinois	ili-ni-wak	men
Idaho	ee-dah-how	behold! the sun coming down the mountain
Iowa	aayahooweewa	sleepy
Kentucky	ken-tah-teh	land of tomorrow
Minnesota	minne-sota	cloudy water
Texas	tiesha	friend

▲ PLAINS SIGN LANGUAGE

Indian - rub back of hand twice

Cheyenne - chop at left index finger

Comanche - imitate motion of snake

Crow - hold fist to forehead, palm out

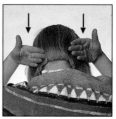
Osage - move hands down back of head

Pawnee - make V sign and extend hand

Nez Percé - move finger under nose

Sioux - hand across neck as if cutting

alone - right hand to the right

buffalo

cannot - move finger along palm and down

horse

bad - make fist then open downwards

moon

opposite

Caught the Enemy   *Eagle Horse*   *He Dog*   *Kills by the Camp*   *Spotted Face*   *Stabber*

△ *Indian names were very meaningful. People were often named after an animal or a special event in their lives (see page 54). These **pictographs** of names were used as signatures by the Sioux.*

SMOKE SIGNALS
were sent by hunters and warriors in the flat, open Plains country, on clear days when no wind blew. By flapping a blanket across the column of smoke from a fire, they made combinations of long and short puffs to tell of the presence of buffalo or the approach of enemies. The system was far from reliable.

▷ *A Plains Indian girl and a Nez Percé boy would have been able to speak to one another using sign language.*

◁ *In the early 19th century, Sequoya developed a writing system for the Cherokee language. His alphabet contained 85 characters and each one represented a syllable, or unit from which a word is made up ('syl-la-ble' has three units).*

LANGUAGE WAS SPOKEN, not written. For centuries, North American Indians saw no need for alphabets, or for writing down the many stories and traditions they carried around in their heads. Since they did not put their thoughts on paper, they developed fantastic memories and were good at telling stories and making speeches. They used their spoken language in a beautiful, moving way.

SEQUOYA'S CHEROKEE ALPHABET was the only written form of an Indian language. Sequoya (1760–1843) dreamed of giving his people the power of the written word that the Europeans used so well. It was a wild success. Every Cherokee man, woman and child saw how useful reading and writing could be. They began producing their own newspapers in Cherokee and English.

THE MAIN REASON why we know today about the Indians' rich spoken tradition is through the powerful speeches that were made by their chiefs and leaders in **post-contact** times. These speeches were usually about their sadness at losing their lands and at the white man's wasteful ways with nature.

CHIEF SEATTLE made a speech when the city of Seattle was founded on his homelands in 1855. He said:
"There was a time when our people covered the whole land as the waves of the wind-ruffled sea cover its shell-paved floor…Every hillside, every valley, every plain and grove, has been hallowed by some sad or happy event in days long vanished. Even the rocks, which seem to be dumb and dead as they swelter in the sun along the silent shore, thrill with memories of events connected with the lives of my people, and the very dust upon which you now stand… is rich with the blood of our ancestors."

Pictographs were often painted on to hide, or carved into wood and then coloured. Some Northeastern people used this technique to make calendar sticks.

PICTOGRAPHS AND IDEOGRAPHS were used in **pre-contact** times to leave messages or records of things that had happened. Pictographs were little drawings used to represent people, animals, objects or happenings. Ideographs were symbols that stood for abstract ideas like love, longing, hate or sadness.

△ **TRIBAL CHRONICLES** recorded the passing years by focusing on particularly important events that everybody in the group remembered. These might include an outbreak of illness or maybe the sighting of a spectacular comet. Plains peoples painted their chronicles on buffalo hides.

△ **MAKE YOUR OWN CHRONICLE** _____

You will need: plain fabric, paints, paintbrush, pencil

1 Cut the fabric to the shape of a buffalo hide, as shown. Paint it off-white, to look like hide.

2 Make up your own symbols to remind you of important events. Choose one for each week, to sum up the main event of that week, such as playing in a match, getting measles or having a birthday.

3 Paint your symbols on the canvas, starting at the centre of a spiral as shown.

Pictographs used by the Dakota Sioux Indians:

smallpox epidemic　　*shower of meteors*　　*village attacked and inhabitants killed*　　*peace with a rival tribe*　　*successful horse raid*　　*new settlement*

A spiritual life

The unseen spirit world was very real to North American Indians. They believed that the natural world and the spirit world were joined together on Earth. Everything in their lives was controlled by major and minor gods and spirits, from the rising of the sun in the morning to people's success at hunting and the health of their children. They recognized the power of these spirits in everything they did and said.

THREE WORLDS made up the universe, according to Southeastern tribes. They believed that an Upper World, a Lower World and This World were separate but linked. This World, in which man, plants and most animals lived, was a round island resting on water. It hung from the sky on four cords attached at the north, south, west and east. The Upper World was pure, perfect and predictable, and the Lower World was full of chaos and change. This World was balanced between the two. Spirits moved freely between the Worlds and people had the privilege of helping the spirits keep the Worlds in balance.

🏠 MAKE A SPIRIT MASK

You will need: card, masking tape, old newspapers, wallpaper paste, paint, raffia, elastic, glue, Velcro

1 Cut basic shapes for the mask and forehead from card. Make a nose and brows from crumpled paper and tape into place.

2 Tape the forehead to the mask, using crumpled paper to fill it and build the forehead out. Make eye sockets from rings of folded paper, cut card ears and tape into place.

3 Paste strips of paper over the shapes. Allow to dry.

4 Paint the mask white, then add your design in colour. Glue on raffia for the hair.

5 Use card, crumpled paper and papier-mâché to build different mouth shapes. Attach them to the basic mask with Velcro dots.

▽ *The Kwakiutl made masks of the spirit Echo with a different mouth for each creature they believed he could imitate.*

basic mask   *the spirit of Echo itself*   *an eagle or a raven*   *a bear*

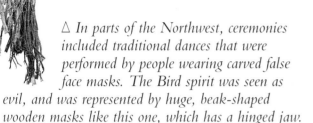

△ *In parts of the Northwest, ceremonies included traditional dances that were performed by people wearing carved false face masks. The Bird spirit was seen as evil, and was represented by huge, beak-shaped wooden masks like this one, which has a hinged jaw.*

STORIES OF HOW THE WORLD BEGAN were told by most tribes. Pueblos believed it was the work of the Spider Grandmother. Some Northwestern tribes thought it was the Raven, while others believed that the world was made by a number of assorted spirits. Their neighbours in the Plateau region saw the world as a clever joke played by their Coyote god. Southeastern people gave the credit to the Master of Breath who lived on high.

VISION QUESTS were an attempt to get personal power from the spirits, instead of relying on the medicine man, or **shaman**. Young men went off alone, fasting, sometimes hurting themselves on purpose and keeping awake until they saw visions. These visions gave them their personal key to getting the spirits' help for the rest of their lives.

⚠ **BLACK ELK** said this about his visions: *"I saw more than I can tell, and I understood more than I saw; for I was seeing in a sacred manner the shapes of all things in the spirit."*

⊞ **FALSE FACE MASKS** were made by medicine men for the Iroquois people. They believed that illness was caused by unkind spirits with horrible faces and no bodies who lived in the forest, spreading sickness. The cure was to confuse the spirits, so medicine men cut mask shapes from living trees and gave them gruesome faces. Then they danced, while wearing the masks, until the bewildered spirits left the area.

RITES OF PASSAGE are **rituals** that mark the important stages in a person's life. For example, many people mark the birth of a child with a naming ceremony, a marriage with a wedding ceremony and a death with a funeral. For most early civilizations, the most important ceremony of all was the celebration of puberty, which is the time when a child becomes an adult. For North American Indians, this meant that young people no longer needed to be protected and could contribute fully to their group.

△ **A BABY WAS NAMED** a few days after it was born. A respected warrior would be paid, usually in horses, to name the baby. The child's given name often reflected some glorious action in the warrior's past, but it would be changed when the child made a mark for itself and earned its own name.

△ *Southwestern Hopi Indians wore* **kachina** *masks when they performed certain special festive dances.*

MAKE A KACHINA DOLL

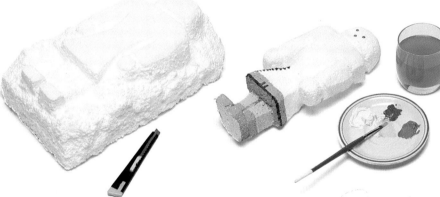

You will need: polystyrene block, PVA paints, sandpaper, craft knife, raffia, coloured wool

1 Draw an outline on the polystyrene.

2 Carve out the shape carefully with a craft knife, as shown. When the basic shape is cut, use sandpaper to smooth and round off the edges.

3 Paint a face and clothes on your doll, and add your own designs. Decorate waist and wrists with raffia and coloured wool.

BECOMING AN ADULT was tough. Boys as young as 10 would have to prove that they were made of strong stuff. In the Yuma tribe, boys had to run 15 to 25 kilometres a day for four days, with no sleep or food. Girls had to lie still, face down, on a bed of warm sand for four days while friends and relatives made long speeches.

MARRIAGE was mostly a free choice. Among Pueblo Indians, the bridegroom moved in with his wife's family, but could be sent home to his mother if things did not work out. Husbands and wives were expected to be faithful while their marriage lasted. Bridegrooms were expected to weave their bride's wedding clothes.

Tawa, who was associated with the sun

Sio Calako, a giant spirit

KACHINAS were spirits that for six months of the year were thought to inhabit the bodies of kachina impersonators – men who wore special masks and costumes in Pueblo ceremonies. Through these men, people asked for help from the spirit world. Children were given kachina dolls to help them understand the spirit world and identify kachinas.

Eototo, chief of the kachinas

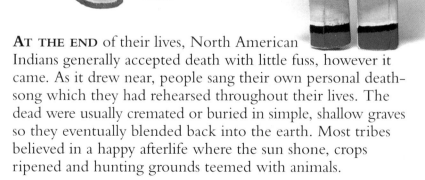

AT THE END of their lives, North American Indians generally accepted death with little fuss, however it came. As it drew near, people sang their own personal death-song which they had rehearsed throughout their lives. The dead were usually cremated or buried in simple, shallow graves so they eventually blended back into the earth. Most tribes believed in a happy afterlife where the sun shone, crops ripened and hunting grounds teemed with animals.

SMOKING THE PIPE OF PRAYER was one of the most important rites. People smoked a mixture of tobacco and sweet-smelling herbs in a ceremonial pipe. They believed that the smoke was the very breath of prayer, and the pipe itself was seen as a sacred pathway to the spirit world.

Give and take

North American Indians respected nature and so did not take from it without giving something back. They hunted and fished carefully and cut down few live trees, taking only what they needed. They had a special relationship with nature and understood how important it was not to upset nature's delicate balance.

THE INDIANS UNDERSTOOD the world around them and knew what to expect from it. They watched the seasons come and go. They observed the movements of the stars and planets, the life cycle of plants and trees, and the regular habits and breeding seasons of the animals they hunted. They were not particularly curious to know why these things happened, because the answer was obvious to them. Everything was the work of the spirit world.

ⓘ MAKE A SAND PAINTING

 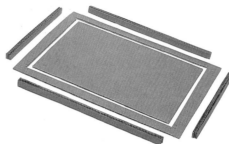 

You will need: sand (silver sand is finer and easier to use than builder's sand), water-based powder paints in a variety of colours, bowl, stirring stick, thick card, pencil, craft knife, glue

1 Mix paint and a little water into a thick paste in the bowl. Add a cup of sand and stir.

2 Spoon the mixture on to a piece of card and leave in a warm place until completely dry. Repeat for all colours.

3 Make the sand painting tray. Measure and cut the card as shown. Make each side piece by cutting three identical strips of card and sticking them together.

4 Work out the space between the base and surround by measuring the thickness of the sides. Wedge each side into place.

5 Fill your tray with uncoloured sand, about half a centimetre deep. Taking a pinch of one of your coloured sands, trickle it carefully on to the base.

HEALING THE SICK was one of the main tasks of the shaman, or medicine man or woman. Healing was done with herbs and with a lot of ritual, which in itself can often help a sick person to feel better. The Indians discovered the healing properties of plants such as willow bark (which contains salicylic acid, the main ingredient of today's aspirin). Their remedies worked so well that the American government officially accepted 170 of them.

◁ *The Navajo used sacred sand paintings as their main way of treating sick people. They believed that a person's illness would be healed by the symbols in the sand. When a painting was finished, it was immediately rubbed out.*

A CHEROKEE STORY told that people upset the spirits of the animals because they killed them for food and crowded them out of their habitats. The animals took their revenge on humans by creating disease and sickness. But the spirits of the plants, who were people's friends, decided to help out. Each single plant, from the tallest trees down to the tiniest creeping mosses, agreed to produce a remedy that would fight and cure one of the diseases.

6 Gradually build up the different colours in your design. It is important to plan the design and colours before you begin. The design shown here is based on a sacred Navajo sand painting used to cure a sick baby. It would have been painted on the floor of the family hogan spread with a smooth layer of uncoloured sand.

SAND PAINTINGS were made by medicine men or women. Clean sand was spread for the background and then a coloured sand picture was created on top. The sick person had to sit or lie on the painting. After the ceremony, when the shaman had prayed and chanted, people took a pinch of the sand. They believed it had healing powers and could be used as a headache cure or a lucky charm. The rest of the sand was swept on to blankets and left near the sick person's house.

Looking back

Finding out how people lived in the past needs careful detective work, especially when they left no written records of their lives.

THE FIRST STEP is to gather evidence. To investigate North American Indian life, we can listen to the stories and memories of present-day Indians, passed down from one generation to the next. We can take account of travellers' tales from the earliest European explorers, who wrote about and drew what they saw. We can also investigate the findings of archaeologists, who study the objects that people have left behind, and anthropologists, who study how people lived their daily lives.

▽ *This model is based on the archaeological dig at the Koster site in western Illinois. The site is named after the farmers on whose land the first finds were made in 1969. Since then, experts have dug through evidence of 15 settlements. The oldest, at about 10 metres below the present level, dates from 9,000 years ago.*

marker post

sorting table

top soil

levels of soil marked to make a vertical grid

THE SECOND STEP is to use the evidence we have found to draw conclusions about how North American Indians lived many hundreds of years ago. This task may be complicated by the fact that different experts sometimes reach different conclusions. Their pictures of the past do not always match up, and every generation looks at history from a slightly different angle. The past is always much more complicated than we think.

top level

horizontal grid
marked on the
surface of the soil

A GRID SYSTEM helps archaeologists to sort out the objects they have found. They push marker posts into the ground and mark off the levels of soil in layers, so there are vertical lines through the whole site. They mark a horizontal grid on the surface, numbering the lines like grid references on a map. Every object is recorded with a reference to show where it was found and to which layer it belonged.

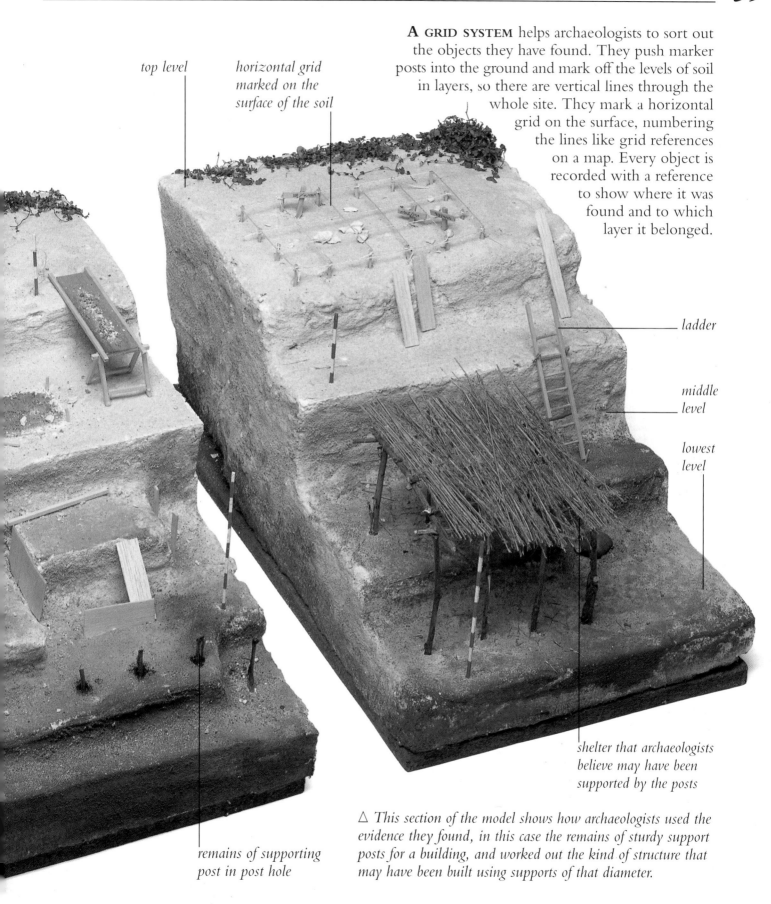

ladder

middle
level

lowest
level

shelter that archaeologists
believe may have been
supported by the posts

remains of supporting
post in post hole

△ *This section of the model shows how archaeologists used the evidence they found, in this case the remains of sturdy support posts for a building, and worked out the kind of structure that may have been built using supports of that diameter.*

Post-contact times

North American Indian history spans about 50,000 years. During this time a number of different cultures have come and gone. But the greatest upheaval the Indians have ever faced was the coming of the Europeans, starting with Christopher Columbus in 1492. The Spanish, the Dutch, the French and the English arrived in waves. They landed in the east and gradually pushed the Indians further and further west. These new settlers came with guns and they believed the rich, fertile land was theirs for the taking, so they took it.

△ Chief Red Horse, of the Sioux Indians, drew a series of pictographs representing the Battle of Little Bighorn. This pictograph shows the climax of the battle.

THE NATIONAL POLICY STATEMENT made by the American government towards North American Indians in 1787 was full of promises that were soon broken. It said: *"The utmost good faith shall always be observed towards the Indians; their lands and property shall never be taken from them without their consent."*

THE NEW SETTLERS, whose ancestors had arrived from Europe, took territorial control from the Indians starting in the east, and gradually acquired land further to the west. Between 1776 and 1854, the North American Indians were forced back until all their land was lost, and by 1912, 48 states of America had been founded.

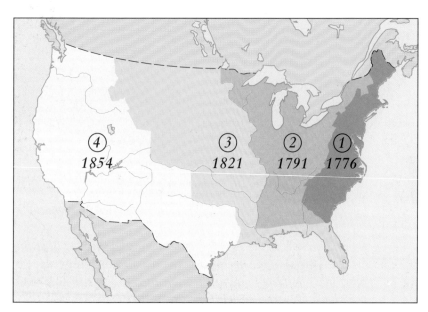

④ 1854   ③ 1821   ② 1791   ① 1776

◁ This map shows the stages by which the new settlers took territory over from the North American Indians. Each shaded area shows the land acquired by the date shown.

△ *Custer hoped to improve his reputation with a victory over the Sioux Indians. His troops, however, were defeated and he was killed.*

CUSTER was an American General who led his troops into many battles with the Plains Indians over their land and traditional hunting grounds. He grew to respect the North American Indian people. He published a book about his life in 1874 called *My Life on the Plains*. In it he wrote: *"When the soil which he has claimed and hunted over for so long a time is demanded by this... insatiable monster (civilization) there is no appeal; he must yield, or it will roll mercilessly over him, destroying as it advances. Destiny seems to have so willed it, and the world nods its approval."*

TWO YEARS LATER, in 1876, General Custer and one third of his cavalry regiment were killed in the Battle of Little Bighorn. They fought against the Sioux nation under its chief, Crazy Horse. This was the Indians' greatest victory against the advancing enemies, but in the end it changed nothing.

▷ *Zuni Indians still produce intricate jewellery from precious stones and silver. This picture was taken in the Southwest in 1970.*

THE LAST OF THE INDIAN WARS was at Wounded Knee in South Dakota in March 1890, when American troops opened fire on a band of Sioux men, women and children, killing 200 of them. In 1890, the last of the heartbroken Indian tribes were driven on to reservations, where land was set aside for their use but was run by the American government. In fact, more Indians died of diseases brought by the Europeans, against which they had no defence, than died in the Indian Wars.

TODAY most North American Indians live on reservations in the central and western parts of the United States and Canada. At first, reservation life was a nightmare, with Indian traditions and religions banned and children sent away to school to learn European ways. But Indians are now much more in control of their own lives. They hand on knowledge of their rich and varied traditions, and reach out to everyone with their unique record of achievements as a people. The Indians' understanding of the environment and nature's delicate balance is of great importance to people all over the world today.

Glossary

Algonquian tribes A group of Northeastern tribes who spoke the Algonquian language. There were about 50 different versions of this language.

anthropologist A person who studies the origins, development and behaviour of people.

archaeologist A person who studies remains from the past, such as buildings and possessions.

bola A rope with a weight such as a stone attached to it. Bolas were thrown as hunting weapons to bring down prey by entangling its legs, or whirled around to knock birds out of the sky.

buckskin Animal hide scraped and softened until it looks and feels like the soft, supple skin of a male deer.

canoe A thin, lightweight boat with pointed ends and no keel. Canoes are pushed through the water by paddles.

chickee A hut on stilts with no walls.

chronicle A record of events, described in the order in which they happened.

civilization A developed and organized group or nation of people.

clan A group of related families.

counting coup A North American Indian way of judging a warrior's bravery. The warrior had to come face to face with his enemy and touch him with a coup stick.

culture A group of people living at a particular time in history, who believe in the same things and share a way of life.

hogan A hexagonal or octagonal hut made from a log framework and plastered with mud.

Ice Age Throughout history there have been a number of Ice ages, when the world's climate became very cold and parts of Northern Europe, Asia and America were completely covered in ice. The last Ice age, which was fairly mild, lasted about 40,000 years and ended about 11,000 years ago.

ideograph A sign that is written down and used to represent an idea such as love or hate.

igloo A dome-shaped house built from blocks of hard snow or ice.

Iroquois tribes A group of Northeastern tribes who spoke the Iroquois language. These tribes were known in post-contact times as the five nations.

kachina Spirits of nature represented by a religious or ceremonial mask or doll-like figure.

lacrosse A team game that originated among North American Indians. It was played using sticks with rawhide nets at the end, and a ball made from hair and hide.

moccasins Shoes or boots made out of animal hide.

New World The continents of the western hemisphere: North and South America, the nearby islands, and Australia. It was known as "New" because these were the last parts of the world to be discovered by European explorers.

nomadic The way of life of groups of people who have no fixed home and wander from place to place looking for food and shelter.

Old World The continents of the eastern hemisphere: Europe, Asia and Africa. These were the parts of the world from which explorers set sail on voyages of discovery to areas that they called the New World.

pictograph A sign that is written down and used to represent a person or an object.

post-contact The time in North American Indian history after the native population had come face to face with explorers and settlers from Europe and the rest of the Old World.

potlatch A Northwestern American Indian ceremonial feast at which many gifts are given to the guests to demonstrate the host's wealth and generosity.

pre-contact The long period of time before North American Indians had any contact with people from other lands.

pueblo A village of terraced mud houses, sometimes built into the sides of hills.

rawhide Stiff animal hide that has been cleaned but is untreated.

ritual A set, ceremonial way of doing something or celebrating an important event.

roach A stiff tuft of animal hair tied on top of the head, worn for decoration.

shaman A man or woman who was believed to have a close relationship with the spirit world. People believed shamans could explain the workings of the gods to them, and make their prayers heard.

symbol A visible sign that represents an invisible idea.

tepee A portable, cone-shaped tent of animal skin or bark set over a wooden framework.

terrain The physical characteristics of an area, such as its mountains, rivers, vegetation.

tomahawk A war club with a rounded end. The word was later used to describe war-axes, introduced by Europeans.

totem pole A post that was carved and painted with symbols (usually animals) to represent family members and ancestors.

travois A trailing sledge, pulled along by dogs or, later, by horses and used for carrying possessions and people.

tribe A large group of related families.

wampum Small, white, cylindrical beads made from polished shells and used as money and expensive jewellery.

wickiup A cone-shaped hut made from grasses and rushes over a wooden frame.

wigwam A dome-shaped home made from wooden poles covered with reed or bark mats.

Index